FAITH
ALIVE®
Christian Resources

2850 Kalamazoo Avenue SE
Grand Rapids, Michigan 49560

ISBN 1-59255-215-3

10 9 8 7 6 5 4 3 2 1

Preface

How many specific lessons do you remember from Sunday school? Probably not very many. But how about the songs you sang in Sunday school? Do you remember the words to "If You're Happy and You Know It," "Away in a Manger," or "Oh, Be Careful, Little Eyes"?

Choosing songs for children to sing is a priestly task. It is priestly because the chooser of the song puts words into the mouths of children—words that are used in speaking to or of God. These sung words become the foundational expressions of children's faith. The pairing of text and music is powerful—so powerful that St. Augustine wavered between encouraging singing and wanting to stop the practice altogether. But singing has been an important way to praise God since the dawn of time (Job 38:7), and because it's a good learning tool and an enjoyable activity, we use it for the glory of God.

Sing With Me is connected to a curriculum for children that follows a long line of church school curricula incorporating music to help children learn. *Walk With Me,* a new Sunday school curriculum launched in 2004 by Faith Alive Christian Resources, uses hundreds of songs throughout its materials for children in preschool through grade 8, and *Sing with Me* follows up by compiling many of those songs—and more—into a single songbook. *Sing With Me* is therefore a great resource not only for Sunday school but also for congregational worship, Christian day schools, home schools, families, and even young piano students.

Approximately half of the songbook is made up of a wide range of songs from the various age levels of the *Walk With Me* curriculum, including "God's Not Dead," "Joshua Fought the Battle of Jericho," "Praise to the Infant King," "Amigos de Cristo," "Every Move I Make," "Angels We Have Heard on High," "One, Two, Three, Jesus Loves Me," and many others. To help connect this songbook to *Walk With Me,* we have chosen to use the categories used in the curriculum: *Hello, Know, Grow,* and *Show. Hello* is the opening or gathering time, *Know* focuses on teaching God's story from creation to re-creation, *Grow* is about our growing relationship to God, and *Show* is about taking the gospel message out into the world. You will also find subsections that correlate to the elements of a worship service. (For more information on *Walk With Me,* call 1-800-333-8300 or visit www.FaithAliveResources.org.)

The committee that gathered to expand on the *Walk With Me* selections sought to provide a balance between songs that are joyful and songs that are confessions or that deal seriously with struggles kids face in this increasingly complex world. We looked for songs that are energetic and playful as well as reflective, songs that kids can sing for fun and songs that can be included in worship, songs that represent the culture we live in and songs that incorporate the languages and styles of other cultures. Overriding our desire for breadth, however, was a desire for depth—songs that are biblically and theologically accurate while serving the priestly function of faith development.

This edition of *Sing With Me* is for the singer and includes simplified accompaniments where appropriate. For full accompaniments see the *Sing With Me* Leader's Edition.

Special thanks are due to Sherry Merz, who chose the bulk of the music for the *Walk With Me* curriculum that serves as the spine for this collection. We are also grateful for the work of the *Sing With Me* committee: Scott Bosscher, Kathleen Hart Brumm, Sherry Merz, Janice Postma, Tim TenClay, Greg Scheer, Nancy Vermeer, and David Vroege. In addition we thank the editorial staff at Faith Alive Christian Resources, with particular thanks to Lynn Setsma and Kristie Schrotenboer for securing copyrights, to Emily Brink for editorial assistance with the music, and to Kathryn Tae Ritsema for editing and administrative assistance throughout the project.

Joyce Borger, editor

Contents

Be Still and Know

Additional stanzas:

I am the Lord that healeth thee. *(x3)*

In you, O Lord, I put my trust. *(x3)*

Words and music: anonymous, based on Psalm 46:10, 7:1; Exodus 15:26; arr. Norma de Waal Malefyt, 1992.
Arr. © 1994, CRC Publications

2 Clap Your Hands

Round

1 Clap your hands, all you peo-ple; shout un-to God with a voice of tri-umph! Clap your hands, all you peo-ple; shout un-to God with a voice of praise! Ho-san-na! Ho-san-na! Shout un-to God with a voice of tri-umph! Praise him! Praise him! Shout un-to God with a voice of praise!

2 Clap your hands, all you peo-ple; Christ has as-cend-ed in-to hea-ven! Clap your hands, all you peo-ple; Christ has as-cend-ed with shouts of joy! Ho-san-na! Ho-san-na! Christ has as-cend-ed in-to hea-ven! Praise him! Praise him! Christ has as-cend-ed with shouts of joy!

Words: st. 1, Carol Owens (BJ), Jimmy Owens (BJ), 1972; st. 2, Bert Polman
Music: Carol Owens (BJ), Jimmy Owens (BJ); harm. Charlotte Larsen

CLAP YOUR HANDS

Come, Let Us Worship and Bow Down

3

Words and music: Dave Doherty

4 Uyai Mose/Come, All You People

Words: st. 1, Alexander Gondo (20th cent., Zimbabwe), tr. I-to Loh; st. 2-3,
With One Voice (1995)
Music: Alexander Gondo; arr. John L. Bell

56 56 56 7
UYAI MOSE

5 Come, Now Is the Time to Worship

Come, now is the time to wor - ship; come, now is the time to give your heart. Come just as you are to wor - ship; come just as you are be-fore your God.

Words and music: Brian Doerkson
© 1998, Vineyard Songs (UK/EIRE) (PRS), admin. in North America by Music Services. All rights reserved.
    Used by permission.

6 Here I Am to Worship

1 Light of the world, you stepped down in-to dark-ness,
2 King of all days, oh so high-ly ex-al-ted,

o-pened my eyes, let me see.
glo-rious in heav-en a-bove.

Beau-ty that made this heart a-dore you,
Hum-bly you came to the earth you cre-a-ted,

hope of a life spent with you.
all for love's sake be-came poor.

So here I am to wor-ship; here I am to

Words and music: Tim Hughes
© 2001, Thankyou Music (KWY) (PRS) (admin. EMI Christian Music Publishing). All rights reserved.
International copyright secured. Used by permission.

7
Yesu Azali Awa/Jesus Christ Is with Us

Ngala   1 Ye - su   a - za - li   a - wa,   Ye - su   a - za - li   a - wa,
English   1 Je - sus   Christ__   is with us,   Je - sus   Christ__   is with us,

Ye - su   a - za - li   a - wa;   na   bi - so.
Je - sus   Christ__   is with us;   he   is   here.

Ye - su   a - za - li   a - wa,   Ye - su   a - za - li   a - wa,
Je - sus   Christ__   is with us,   Je - sus   Christ__   is with us,

Ye - su   a - za - li   a - wa;   na   bi - so.
Je - sus   Christ__   is with us;   he   is   here.

Words: Congolese folk hymn; English tr. Emily R. Brink; Dutch tr. Elly Zuiderveld-Nieman; Korean tr.
    Moongil Cho; Taiwanese tr. Winston Wenn
Music: Congolese folk hymn, traditional

Al - le - lu - ia, al - le - lu - ia, al - le - lu - ia, na Ye - su.
Hal - le - lu - jah, hal - le - lu - jah, hal - le - lu - jah, he is here.

Al - le - lu - ia, al - le - lu - ia, al - le - lu - ia, na Ye - su.
Hal - le - lu - jah, hal - le - lu - jah, hal - le - lu - jah, he is here.

Ngala
2 Biso tokomona ye *(3x)*, na lola. *Repeat*
    Alleluia *(3x)*, na Yesu. *Repeat*

3 Biso tokosepela (3x), na lola. *Repeat*
    Alleluia *(3x)*, na Yesu. *Repeat*

4 Biso tokokutana *(3x)*, na Yesu. *Repeat*
    Alleluia *(3x)*, na Yesu. *Repeat*

5 Biso tokolingana *(3x)*, na lola. *Repeat*
    Alleluia *(3x)*, na Yesu. *Repeat*

English
2 We will see him on his throne *(3x)*, on his throne. *Repeat*
    Hallelujah *(3x)*, on his throne. *Repeat*

3 We'll bring praises to him *(3x)*, on his throne. *Repeat*
    Hallelujah *(3x)*, on his throne. *Repeat*

4 There'll be joy evermore *(3x)*, with the Lord. *Repeat*
    Hallelujah *(3x)*, with the Lord. *Repeat*

5 For his love makes us one *(3x)*, with the Lord. *Repeat*
    Hallelujah *(3x)*, with the Lord. *Repeat*

[Additional texts on following page]

Dutch
1 Jezus Christus is bij ons *(3x)*, hij is hier. *Repeat*
  Halleluja *(3x)*, hij is hier. *Repeat*

2 Eenmaal zullen wij Hem zieu *(3x)*, op zijn troon. *Repeat*
  Halleluja *(3x)*, op Zijn troon. *Repeat*

3 En dan prijzen wij de Heer *(3x)*, op zijn troon. *Repeat*
  Halleluja *(3x)*, op Zijn troon. *Repeat*

4 Er zal eeuwig vreugde zijn (3x), bij de Heer. *Repeat*
  Halleluja *(3x)*, bij de Heer. *Repeat*

5 Want de liefde maakt ons één *(3x)*, bij de Heer. *Repeat*
  Halleluja *(3x)*, bij de Heer. *Repeat*

Korean
1 Yesu oo ree wah hahm keah *(3x)*, yogi yeah! *Repeat*
  Hallelujah *(3x)*, yogi yeah! *Repeat*

Taiwanese
1 Jaso Quito kah lahn dee day *(3x)*, ee dee chay! *Repeat*
  Hallelujah *(3x)*, ee dee chay! *Repeat*

Where Two or Three

8

Capo 3

Where two or three are ga-thered in my name, there I will be with them. them. them.

I'll be with them. (I'll be with them.)

I'll be with them. (I'll be with them.)

Fine

D.C. al Fine

Words and music: Bayiga Bayiga
As found in "Thuma Mina," © 1995, *Strube Verlad GmbH,* Munchen and Basileia-Verlag, Basel

9 Say to the Lord, I Love You

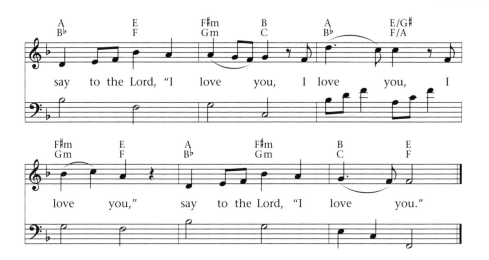

10 Stand Up and Sing

Words and music: Bob and Barbara Dawson
© 1991, Integrity's Hosanna! Music (ASCAP). Used by permission.

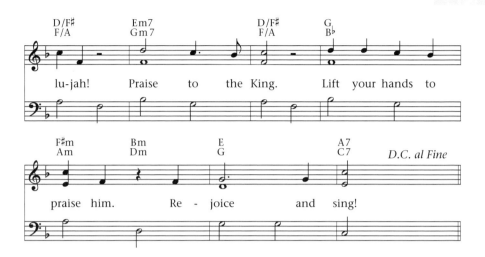

lu-jah! Praise to the King. Lift your hands to

praise him. Re - joice and sing!

D.C. al Fine

Come, Let Us Gather

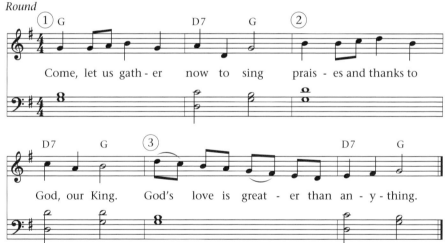

Round

Come, let us gath-er now to sing prais-es and thanks to

God, our King. God's love is great - er than an - y - thing.

Orff or other C instrument patterns

Triangle or soprano glockenspiel   *Alto xylophone*

Alto glockenspiel   *Bass xylophone*

Words and music: traditional; arr. Richard L. Van Oss, 1991
Arr. © 1994, CRC Publications

12 Step by Step

O God, you are my God, and I will ev-er praise you. O God, you are my God, and I will ev-er praise you. I will seek you in the morn-ing, and I will learn to walk in your ways. And step by step you'll lead me, and I will

Words and music: David Strasser p/k/a/Beaker

Come, Lord Jesus 13

1 Come, Lord Je - sus. Come, Lord Je - sus.
2 Come, O Prince of Peace. Come, O Prince of Peace.
3 Our hearts are o - pen. Our hearts are o - pen.
4 Come, Im - man - u - el. Come, Im - man - u - el.

Come, Lord Je - sus;
Come, O Prince of Peace;   come and be born in our hearts.
Our hearts are o - pen;
Come, Im - man - u - el;

14 All Creatures of Our God and King

Words: Francis of Assisi, 1225; tr. William H. Draper, 1910
Music: *Auserlesen Catholische Geistliche Kirchengesang*, Cologne, 1623

LM with alleluias
LASST UNS ERFREUEN

Alleluia Canon

15

Alleluia, alleluia, alleluia, alleluia.

Music: W. A. Mozart, 1756-1791; from *Exultate, Jubilate*, adapt.; arr. Janice Postma.
Arr. © 2006, Faith Alive Christian Resources

16 I Will Celebrate

May be sung as a round

Come, Praise the Lord 17

Capo 3

1 Day or night, (day or night) we will praise the Lord. Day or night, (day or night) we will praise the Lord. Day or night, (day or night) we will praise the Lord.
2 Rain or shine, (rain or shine) we will praise the Lord. Rain or shine, (rain or shine) we will praise the Lord. Rain or shine, (rain or shine) we will praise the Lord.
3 Big or small, (big or small) we will praise the Lord. Big or small, (big or small) we will praise the Lord. Big or small, (big or small) we will praise the Lord.
4 Soft or loud, (soft or loud) we will praise the Lord. Soft or loud, (soft or loud) we will praise the Lord. Soft or loud, (soft or loud) we will praise the Lord.

All you chil-dren, come, praise the Lord!

Words and music: Stephen Elkins

18 Every Move I Make

Words and music: David Ruis

19 God Is Good All the Time

God is good all the time. He put a
song of praise in this heart of mine. God is
good all the time. Through the
dark - est night his light will shine. God is
good. God is good all the time.

3rd time to Coda

Words and music: Don Moen and Paul Overstreet
© 1995, Integrity's Hosanna! Music (ASCAP) and Scarlet Moon Music, Inc. (BMI). Used by permission.

leave you ... nor for - sake you, ... and his

Word is true. God is time.

D.S al Coda ⊕ *Coda*

20 Awesome God

Our God is an awe - some God. He reigns from

heav - en a - bove with wis - dom, pow'r, and love. Our

God is an awe - some God!

Words and music: Rich Mullins

God Is So Good

21

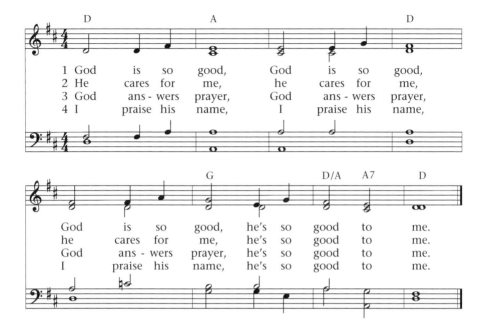

```
1 God    is    so   good,   God   is    so   good,
2 He     cares for  me,     he    cares for  me,
3 God    ans-wers prayer,   God   ans-wers prayer,
4 I      praise his name,   I     praise his name,

God    is    so   good,   he's  so   good  to   me.
he     cares for  me,     he's  so   good  to   me.
God    ans-wers prayer,   he's  so   good  to   me.
I      praise his name,   he's  so   good  to   me.
```

Stanza 1 in these languages:

Korean: Cho-u-shin Ha-na-nim, Cho-u-shin Ha-na-nim,
            cham cho-u-shin, na ui Ha-na-nim.

Spanish: Dios es muy bue-no, Dios es muy bue-no,
            Dios es muy bue-no, es muy bue-no pa-ra mi.

Swahili: Mungu yu M-we-ma, Mungu yu M-we-ma,
            Mungu yu M-we-ma, Yu m-we-ma Kwan-gu.

Descant

Words and music: traditional; desc. Susan Nipp

22 God Is Great

23 God Is the Rock

Who is the rock ex-cept our God? God is the rock!

Who is God be-sides the Lord? God is the rock!

Who is the rock? God is the rock! Who is the rock? God

is the rock! Who is the rock? God is the rock!

God is the rock! God is the rock of our sal-va-tion.

Hallelujah! Praise the Lamb 24

Capo 3

Hal - le - lu - jah! Praise the Lamb! Hal - le -

lu - jah! Praise the Lamb! My heart sings this song a-

gain: Hal - le - lu - jah! Praise the Lamb!

Words and music: Gary McSpadden, Dawn Thomas, Pamela Thum

25 Ha-Le-La-Le-La-Le-Lu-Jah

Ha - le-la - le - la - le - lu-jah, ha - le-lu - jah to the Lord.

Ha - le-la - le - la - le - lu-jah, praise his name for - ev - er - more.

Ha - le-la - le - la - le - lu-jah. Lift your voice; re - joice and sing.

Ha - le-la - le - la - le - lu-jah to the King of kings.

3rd time to Coda

He is the Ho - ly One, Je - sus, God's

on - ly Son, crown-ing glo - ry of all cre - a - tion.

Clap your hands in ce - le - bra-tion.

2nd time D.C. al Coda

Ha - le - la - le - la - le - lu - jah to the King of kings.

26 He's Got the Whole World

1 He's got the whole world in his hands. He's got the whole world in his hands. He's got the whole world in his hands. He's got the whole world in his hands.

2 He's got the little tiny baby in his hands. *(3x)*
He's got the whole world in his hands.

3 He's got you and me, brother, in his hands. *(3x)*
He's got the whole world in his hands.

4 He's got you and me, sister, in his hands. *(3x)*
He's got the whole world in his hands.

5 He's got everybody here in his hands. *(3x)*
He's got the whole world in his hands.

Words and music: African-American spiritual   WHOLE WORLD

Santo, santo, santo, mi corazón/ Holy, Holy, Holy, My Heart

27

Spanish San - to, san - to, san - to,   mi cor - a -
English Ho - ly, ho - ly, ho - ly,   my heart, my
Dutch Hei - lig, hei - lig, hei - lig,   mijn hart brengt
French Dieu saint, Dieu saint, Dieu saint,   mon coeur, mon
Korean Gaw - rohk, gaw - rohk, gaw - rohk,   nah - ruhl Ju -

zón te a - do - ra!   Mi cor - a - zón te
heart a - dores you!   My heart pours out my
U de e - re!   Van har - te loof ik
coeur t'a - do - re.   Mon coeur le dit, mon
neem - ke drim nee-dah.   Nay - ga Ju - neem chan

sa - be de - cir: san - to e - res Se - ñor.
praise to you;   you are ho - ly, Lord.
U - we Naam;   hei - lig bent U, Heer.
coeur s'en ré - jouit: tu es saint, mon Dieu.
yahng hop - nee - dah;   gaw - rohk hash in, Ju - neem.

Words and music: Spanish traditional; English tr. *Sing! A New Creation* (2001); Dutch tr. Robert DeMoor; French tr. Otto Selles; Korean tr. In Soon Gho; arr. Kathryn Tae Ritsema
© 2001, CRC Publications; arr. © 2006, Faith Alive Christian Resources

28 Holy, Holy, Holy! Lord God Almighty

1 Ho-ly, ho-ly, ho-ly! Lord God Al-might-y!
2 Ho-ly, ho-ly, ho-ly! All the saints a-dore thee,
3 Ho-ly, ho-ly, ho-ly! Though the dark-ness hide thee,
4 Ho-ly, ho-ly, ho-ly! Lord God Al-might-y!

Ear-ly in the morn-ing our song shall rise to thee;
cast-ing down their gold-en crowns a-round the glass-y sea;
though the eye made blind by sin thy glo-ry may not see,
All thy works shall praise thy name, in earth and sky and sea;

ho-ly, ho-ly, ho-ly! mer-ci-ful and might-y,
cher-u-bim and ser-a-phim fall-ing down be-fore thee,
on-ly thou art ho-ly; there is none be-side thee,
ho-ly, ho-ly, ho-ly! mer-ci-ful and might-y,

God in three per-sons, bless-ed Trin-i-ty!
who wert and art and ev-er-more shalt be.
per-fect in power, in love, and pu-ri-ty.
God in three per-sons, bless-ed Trin-i-ty!

Words: Reginald Heber, 1827, alt.
Music: John B. Dykes, 1861; arr. Greg Scheer.
Arr. © 2006, Faith Alive Christian Resources.

11 12 12 10
NICAEA

Hosanna 29

1 Ho-san-na, ho-san-na, ho-san-na in the high - est. Ho-san-na, ho-san-na, ho-san-na in the high - est. Lord, we lift up your name with hearts full of praise. Be ex-alt-ed, O Lord, my God. Ho-san-na in the high - est.

2 Glo-ry, glo-ry, glo-ry to the King of kings! Glo-ry, glo-ry, glo-ry to the King of kings! Lord, we lift up your name with hearts full of praise. Be ex-alt-ed, O Lord, my God. Glo-ry to the King of kings!

30 How Majestic Is Your Name

O Lord, our Lord, how ma-jes-tic is your name in all the earth. O Lord, our Lord, how ma-jes-tic is your name in all the earth. O Lord, we praise your name. O Lord, we mag-ni-fy your

Words and music: Michael W. Smith

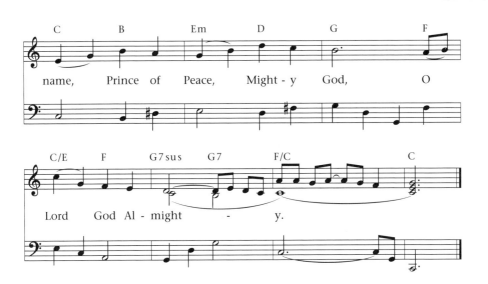

name, Prince of Peace, Might-y God, O
Lord God Al - might - y.

I L-o-v-e, Love You, Lord

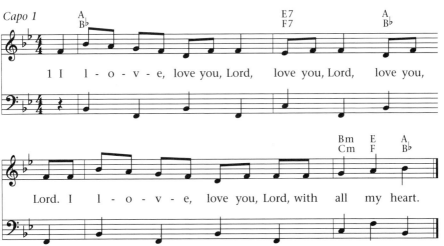

Capo 1

1 I l - o - v - e, love you, Lord, love you, Lord, love you,

Lord. I l - o - v - e, love you, Lord, with all my heart.

Repeat this song 4 more times, each time dropping one letter of the word "l - o - v - e"
and replacing it with a clap (as in "[clap] - o - v - e," etc.).

Words and music: Janet McMahon-Wilson and Ted Wilson; arr. C. Barny Robertson

32 I Have the Joy

Capo 1

1 I have the joy, joy, joy, joy
2 (I have the) love of Je - sus, love of Je - sus
3 (I have the) peace that pass - es un - der - stand - ing
4 (I have the) joy, joy, joy, joy

down in my heart, down in my heart, down in my heart!

I have the joy, joy, joy, joy
I have the love of Je - sus, love of Je - sus
I have the peace that pass - es un - der - stand - ing
I have the joy, joy, joy, joy

down in my heart, down in my heart to stay!

Words and music: traditional; arr. Greg Scheer
Arr. © 2006, Faith Alive Christian Resources

And it's the great-est, grand-est feel-ing, and it's a

feel-ing here to stay! And it's a love that needs re-
peace

joy

veal-ing, so I just want to say: I have the

33 I Will Call Upon the Lord

34 Te exaltaré, mi Dios, mi Rey/ I Will Exalt My God, My King

I will ex-alt my God, my King; I will praise your
Te e-xal-ta-ré, mi Dios, mi Rey, y ben-de-ci-

name for-ev-er. I will ex-alt your
ré tu nom-bre. E-ter-na-men-te y

name for-ev-er; ev-ery day I'll praise your ho-ly name.
pa-ra siem-pre, ca-da dí-a te ben-de-ci-ré.

I will praise your name for-ev-er; I will ex-
Y a-la-ba-ré tu nom-bre e-ter-na-

alt your name for-ev-er. Lord our God,
men-te y pa-ra siem-pre. Gran-de es

Words: Psalm 145:1-3; versified by Casiodoro Cardenas, 1979; composite translation
Music: Casiodoro Cardenas, 1979; arr. Raquel Mora Martínez, 1979

ECUADOR

you are great and wor-thy of the high-est praise and hon -
Je - ho - vá y dig -no de su - pre-ma a - la - ban -

or, for your great - ness is far be - yond us;
za; y su gran - de - za es in - es - cru - ta - ble;

ev - ery day I'll praise your ho - ly name.
ca - da dí - a te ben - de - ci - ré.

Woodblock

Castanets

Tambourine

Sticks

35 I'm So Glad Jesus Lifted Me

1 I'm   so   glad
2 Satan had me bound;   Je - sus lift - ed me.
3 When I was in trouble,

I'm   so   glad
Satan had me bound;   Je - sus lift - ed me.
When I was in trouble,

I'm   so   glad
Satan had me bound;   Je - sus lift - ed me,   sing - ing
When I was in trouble,

glo - ry, hal - le - lu - jah!   Je - sus lift - ed me.

Words and music: African-American spiritual   JESUS LIFTED ME

Imela/We Thank You

36

Ibo 1 I - me - la, i - me - la,
English 1 We thank you, thank you, God.

i - me - la, O - ka - ka. I - me - la.
We thank you, thank you, God. We thank you.

Chi - ne - ke. I - me - la. On - y'o - ma.
You are good. We thank you. You are good.

2 We love you, love you, God. *(2x)*
   We love you. You are good. *(2x)*

3 We praise you, praise you, God. *(2x)*
   We praise you. You are good. *(2x)*

Words: traditional
Music: © 1990, Christ Church Gospel Band, Uwani-Engu; as taught by Mrs. Unoaku Ekwegbalu.
Arr. © 1990, Wild Goose Resource Group, Iona Community, Scotland. GIA Publications, Inc., exclusive
   North American agent. All rights reserved. Used by permission.

37 Just Say Thanks

I want to stop what I'm do-ing and just say "thanks," just say "thanks," just say "thanks." I want to stop what I'm do-ing and just say "thanks! Thank you, God!"

Words and music: Tom McBryde and Janet McMahon-Wilson; arr. C. Barny Robertson

Lord of the Future 38

1 Lord of the fu - ture, Lord of the past,
2 Lord of to - mor - row, Lord of to - day,

Lord of our lives, we a - dore you.
Lord o - ver all, you are worth - y.

Lord of for - e - ver, Lord of our hearts,
Lord of cre - a - tion, Lord of all truth,

we give all praise to you. you.
we give all praise to

39 Lord, I Lift Your Name on High

Lord, I lift your name on high;

Lord, I love to sing your prais - es.

I'm so glad you're in my life;

I'm so glad you came to save us.

You came from heav - en to earth to show the

Words and music: Rick Founds

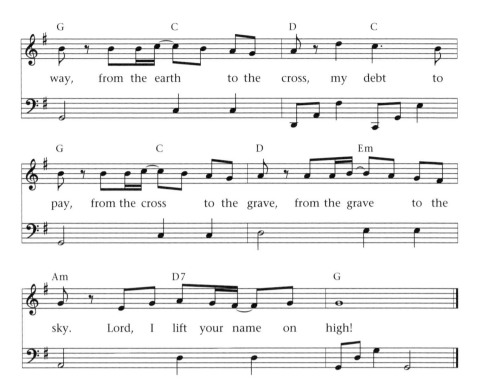

way, from the earth to the cross, my debt to

pay, from the cross to the grave, from the grave to the

sky. Lord, I lift your name on high!

40 My God Is So Great

Capo 3

D
F

(hold up arms and flex muscles)
My God is so great, so strong and so might-y! There's

A7
C7

D
F

Fine

(shake head "no")
noth-ing my God can-not do! (clap, clap)

G
Bb

D
F

(hands form mountain peak above head) *(wiggle fingers from left to right)*
The moun-tains are his, the riv-ers are his, the

A7
C7

D
F

D.C. al Fine

(fingers make twinkling stars)
stars are his hand-i-work too.

Words and music: children's folk song; arr. Charlotte Larsen
Arr. © 1994, CRC Publications

Cantad al Señor/O Sing to the Lord   **41**

1 O sing to the Lord, O sing God a new song.
2 O shout to our God, who gave us the Spir - it.
3 For Je - sus is Lord! A - men! Al - le - lu - ia!

O sing to the Lord, O sing God a new song.
O shout to our God, who gave us the Spir - it.
For Je - sus is Lord! A - men! Al - le - lu - ia!

O sing to the Lord, O sing God a new song.
O shout to our God, who gave us the Spir - it.
For Je - sus is Lord! A - men! Al - le - lu - ia!

O sing to our God, O sing to our God.
O sing to our God, O sing to our God.
O sing to our God, O sing to our God.

Spanish words:

1 Cantad al Señor un cántico nuevo. *(3x)* ¡Cantad al Señor, cantad al Señor!

2 Es él que nos da el Espíritu Santo. *(3x)* ¡Cantad al Señor, cantad al Señor!

3 ¡Jesús es Señor! ¡Amen, aleluya! *(3x)* ¡Cantad al Señor, cantad al Señor!

Words and music: Brazilian folk song; st. 1 based on Psalm 98:1; tr. Gerhard M. Cartford
English and Spanish trans. © Gerhard M. Cartford; arr. © Editora Sinodal. Used by permission.

42 Oh, for a Thousand Tongues to Sing

1 Oh, for a thou - sand tongues to sing my
2 He speaks, and, lis - tening to his voice, new

great Re - deem - er's praise, the glo - ries of my
life the dead re - ceive; the mourn - ful, bro - ken

God and King, the tri - umphs of his grace!
hearts re - joice; the hum - ble poor be - lieve.

Additional stanzas:

3 Hear him, you deaf; you voiceless ones,
your loosened tongues employ;
you blind, behold your Savior come;
and leap, you lame, for joy!

4 To God all glory, praise, and love
be now and ever given
by saints below and saints above,
the church in earth and heaven.

Words: Charles Wesley, 1739
Music: Carl G. Glaser, 1828; adapted and arr. Lowell Mason, 1839

CM
AZMON

Praise and Thanksgiving

Round

1 Praise and thanks - giv - ing let ev - ery - one bring
2 All peo - ple, join us and sing out God's praise.
3 May we go out from here shar - ing God's love.

un - to our Fa - ther for ev - ery good thing.
For all his bless - ings your hap - py songs raise.
Help us in com - ing days our faith to prove.

All to - geth - er, joy - ful - ly sing!

Duet for Recorder or other C instrument

Words: st. 1, Alsatian; tr. Edith Lowell Thomas, 1950; st. 2-3, Marie J. Post, 1974
Music: Alsatian round; harm. Dale Grotenhuis, 1985. Recorder desc. Janice Postma
St. 2-3 and harm. © 1987, CRC Publications.
Recorder © 2006, Faith Alive Christian Resources.

10 10 8
LOBET UND PREISET

44 Praise Him, All You Little Children

Additional stanzas:

2 Love him . . .   3 Thank him . . .   4 Serve him . . .

Words: anonymous
Music: Carey Bonner (1859-1938)

Praise to the Lord, the Almighty 45

1 Praise to the Lord, the Al - might - y, the King of cre - a - tion! O my soul, praise him, for he is your health and sal - va - tion! Come, all who hear; broth - ers and sis - ters, draw near, join me in glad ad - o - ra - tion!

2 Praise to the Lord! O let all that is in me a - dore him! All that has life and breath, come now with prais - es be - fore him! Let the a - men sound from his peo - ple a - gain. Glad - ly for - ev - er a - dore him!

Words: Joachim Neander, 1680; tr. Catherine Winkworth, 1863
Music: *Erneuerten Gesangbuch*, Stralsund, 1665; arr. Robert Roth, 1989
Arr. © 1989, Robert Roth. Used by permission.

14 14 4 7 8
LOBE DEN HERREN

46 Praise the Lord

Bm

1 Praise the Lord, praise the Lord, for the green-ness
2 Thanks to God, thanks to God, for the gift of
3 Glo - ry to God, glo - ry to God, for the grace of

of the trees, for the beau - ty of the flowers,
friends in Christ, for the church, our house of faith,
Christ, the Son, for the love of par - ent God,

for the blue - ness of the sky, for the great-ness
for the gift of won - drous love, for the gift of
for the com - fort and the strength of the Spir - it,

of the sea. Praise the Lord, praise the Lord,
end - less grace. Thanks to God, thanks to God,
ho - ly God. Glo - ry to God, glo - ry to God,

now and for - ev - er - more.
now and for - ev - er - more.
now and for - ev - er - more.

Words: Nobuaki Hanaoka, Japan, 1980
Music: Japanese traditional melody

What a Mighty God We Serve 47

What a might - y God we serve!

What a might - y God we serve!

An-gels bow be-fore him. Heav-en and earth a - dore him.

What a might - y God we serve.

48 Praise Ye the Lord

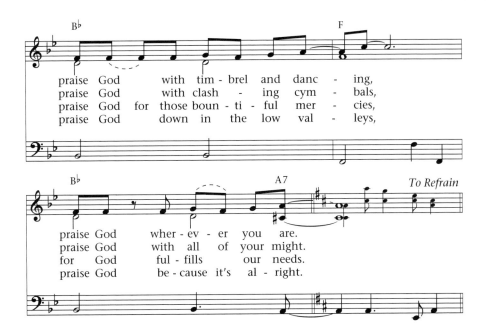

praise God   with   tim - brel   and   danc -   ing,
praise God   with   clash -   ing   cym -   bals,
praise God   for   those boun - ti - ful   mer -   cies,
praise God   down   in   the   low   val -   leys,

praise God   wher - ev - er   you   are.
praise God   with   all   of   your   might.
for   God   ful - fills   our   needs.
praise God   be - cause   it's   al - right.

49 Shout to the Lord

50 Sing Unto the Lord

Sing un-to the Lord a new song. Sing un-to the
Lord all the earth. Sing un-to the Lord a
new song. Sing un-to the Lord all the
earth. For God is great and
great-ly to be praised. God is great and

3rd time to Coda

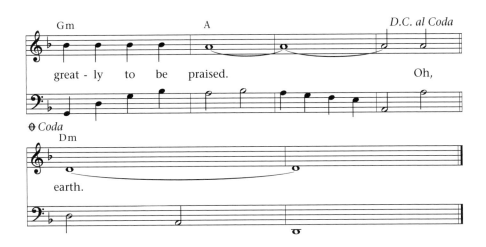

great - ly   to   be   praised.

Oh,

earth.

51 Sing with Hearts

Sing with hearts, sing with souls, dance with joy

Bass xylophone or Stomping stick

to God, to whom we of - fer prais - es, to

whom we sing with glad - ness.

1 Let all our hearts o - pen up to the Lord God.
2 Let all our bod - ies sway to God's mu - sic.
3 Let all our souls shine out with God's beau - ty.

Let all the heav'ns hear how our hearts re - joice.
Let all the earth move with our feet and hands.
Let all cre - a - tion feel our love for God.

Words: Jonathan Malicsi (based on Psalm 100)
Music: Kalinga melody, adapted
Words © 1983, Jonathan Malicsi. Used by permission of Asian Institute for Liturgy and Music.

52 Thank You, Jesus

Capo 3

1 Thank you, Je - sus, thank you, Je - sus,
2 Thank you, Je - sus, thank you, Je - sus,
3 Thank you, Je - sus, thank you, Je - sus,

thanks for fam - i - ly. Thank you, Je - sus,
thank you for our food. Thank you, Je - sus,
thank you for our homes. Thank you, Je - sus,

thank you, Je - sus, thanks for fam - i - ly.
thank you, Je - sus, thank you for our food.
thank you, Je - sus, thank you for our homes.

Refrain

We love to sing and play. We love to

53 Your Everlasting Love

Capo 3

1 Your ev - er-last-ing love is high - er, high - er, high - er than the sky. Your ev - er-last-ing love is high - er, high - er, high - er than the sky,

2 Your ev - er-last-ing love is deep - er, deep - er, deep - er than the sea. Your ev - er-last-ing love is deep - er, deep - er, deep - er than the sea,

3 Your ev - er-last-ing love is reach - ing, reach - ing, reach - ing out to me. Your ev - er-last-ing love is reach - ing, reach - ing, reach - ing out to me,

For the Beauty of the Earth

54

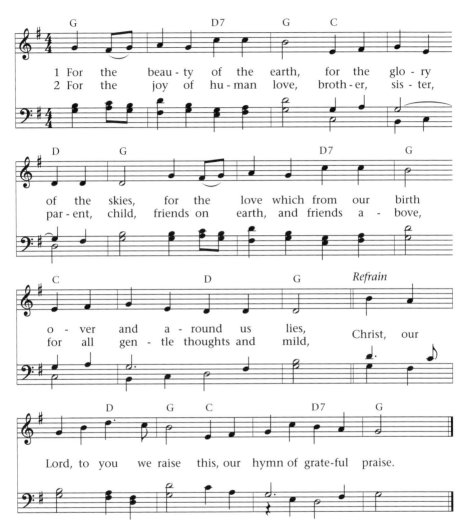

1 For the beau-ty of the earth, for the glo-ry
2 For the joy of hu-man love, broth-er, sis-ter,

of the skies, for the love which from our birth
par-ent, child, friends on earth, and friends a-bove,

o - ver and a - round us lies,
for all gen - tle thoughts and mild,

Refrain

Christ, our

Lord, to you we raise this, our hymn of grate-ful praise.

Words: Folliott S. Pierpont, 1864, alt.
Music: Conrad Kocher, 1838; adapted by William H. Monk, 1861; arr. Robert Roth, 1989
Arr. © 1989, Robert Roth. Used by permission.

77 77 77
DIX

55 Creation Song

1st time Leader, 2nd time All

1 Who made day and who made night? Who made all the

stars so bright? Who made land and sea and sky?

Fish that swim and birds that fly?

All (spoken)

God made day! God made night! He looked at it and

*Optional accompaniment or footstomps

Words: Lynnette Pennings
Music: traditional
Words from *Kids on the Rock!* © 1994, Gospel Light. Used by permission.

said, "ALL RIGHT!"

Additional stanzas with the leader singing each line and everyone else echoing. Everyone speaks the "All" section together:

2 Who made all the plants that grow,
leaves above and roots below?
Who made pine trees tall and green?
Who made corn and lima beans?
All: God made plants, tall and green!
God made corn and lima beans!

3 Who made bats and bumblebees?
Flamingos with their knobby knees?
Leopard cubs and elephants?
Wolves that howl and dogs that pant?
All: God made bats! God made bees!
God made dogs and itchy fleas!

4 Who made people dark and light?
Gave us earth and sky so bright?
Who wants us to treat it right?
Who loves us both day and night?
All: God loves us, dark and light!
God loves us both day and night!

5 Who made dinosaurs and whales?
Things with fins and things with tails?
Jellyfish and sharks and bears?
Things with teeth and things with hair?
All: God made sharks! God made bears!
Things that make you say, "Beware!"

6 Who made pigs and lightning bugs?
Mice and moose and slimy slugs?
Who made mold and squirmy worms?
Viruses and tiny germs?
All: God made bugs! God made slugs!
Things that make you (*clap*) say, "UGH!"

56 God Made Everything

Who put the hop in the kang-a-roo? Who put the (*snort*) in the pig? It's true. Who made the cows go moo, moo, moo? God made ev-ery-thing. God made ev-ery-thing. Yes, you know it's true. God made ev-ery-thing, and God made me and you.

God Made Me, Every Part You See
57

Let the children point to the appropriate parts of their bodies.
They might also skip, hop, or dance to the song.

Words: Daniel Burrow
Music: unknown

58 Many and Great

Words: Joseph R. Renville, c. 1846; tr. Philip Frazier, 1929
Music: traditional Dakota

LACQUIPARLE

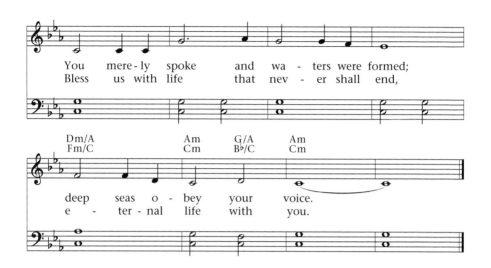

You mere-ly spoke and wa - ters were formed;
Bless us with life that nev - er shall end,

Dm/A   Am   G/A   Am
Fm/C   Cm   B♭/C   Cm

deep seas o - bey your voice.
e - ter - nal life with you.

Optional drum pattern

59 That's Good

God said, "That's good, that's good. (spoken) Yes, it's

ver-y, ver-y, ver-y, ver-y good. That's good, that's

good. Yes, it's ver-y, ver-y, ver-y, ver-y good."

1 It all came a-bout in se-ven sim-ple days when
2 It all came a-bout in se-ven sim-ple days when

God cre-a-ted the world. Day
God cre-a-ted the world. Day

60 The Butterfly Song

61 The Lord Is Great

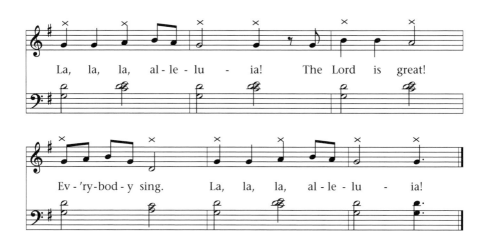

La, la, la, al - le - lu - ia! The Lord is great!

Ev - 'ry-bod - y sing. La, la, la, al - le - lu - ia!

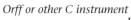

Orff or other C instrument

Last measure

62 This Is My Father's World

1 This is my Fa-ther's world, and to my lis-tening ears all na-ture sings and round me rings the mu-sic of the spheres. This is my Fa-ther's world; I rest me in the thought of rocks and trees, of skies and seas— his hand the won-ders wrought.

2 This is my Fa-ther's world: O let us not for-get that though the wrong is great and strong, God is the rul-er yet. He trusts us with his world, to keep it clean and fair— all earth and trees, all skies and seas, all crea-tures ev-ery-where.

3 This is my Fa-ther's world: he shines in all that's fair; in rus-tling grass I hear him pass— he speaks to me every-where. This is my Fa-ther's world: why should my heart be sad? The Lord is King, let heav-en ring! God reigns; let earth be glad.

Words: Maltbie D. Babcock, 1901; st. 2 revised by Mary Babcock Crawford, 1972.
Music: English; adapted by Franklin L. Sheppard, 1915

SMD
TERRA BEATA

Who Made Ocean, Earth, and Sky

63

The descant may be played by one or two instruments. When using two instruments, alternate every two measures—one playing the question, the other the answer.

Words: Richard Compton, 1921
Music: traditional Finnish melody; arr. Richard L. Van Oss, 1992
Words © 1921, 1948, E. C. Schirmer Music Company. Reprinted by permission of ECS Publishing.
    Arr. © 1994, CRC Publications.

64 Thank You, Lord, for Making Me

Refrain

Let ev-ery-thing that God made say, "Thank you, Lord."

Let ev-ery-thing that God made say, "Thank you, Lord."

4th time to Coda

Let ev-ery-thing that God made say, "Thank you, Lord."

Thank you, Lord, for mak - ing me.

1 The mon-keys in the jun-gle say, "Thank you, Lord."
2 The bears in the woods say, "Thank you, Lord."
3 The ga - tors in the swamp say, "Thank you, Lord."

Words and music: Vince Barlow

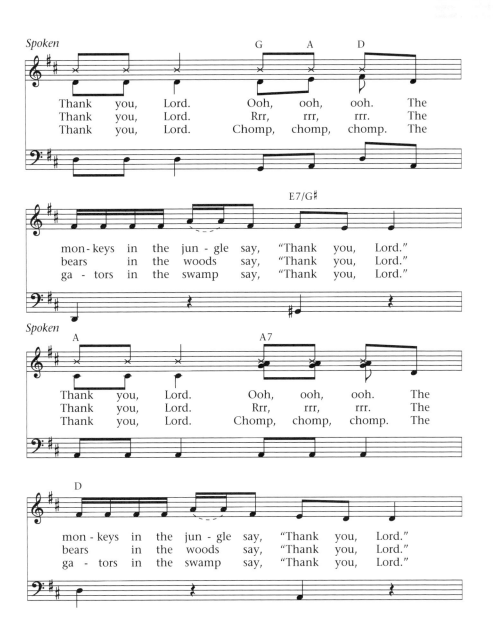

Spoken

Em7   Bm/F♯   Em7

Thank   you,   Lord.   Ooh,   ooh,   ooh.
Thank   you,   Lord.   Rrr,   rrr,   rrr.
Thank   you,   Lord.   Chomp,   chomp,   chomp.

D/A   A   D |1, 2, 3   *To Refrain*
                         G   A7

Thank you, Lord, for mak-ing   me.   Oh   oh,

⊕ *Coda*

D/A   A   D

Thank   you,   Lord,   for   mak - ing   me.

Never Again, Noah! **65**

1 Nev-er a-gain, No-ah, will God say, "Build an ark!"
2 Nev-er a-gain, No-ah, will you build a float-ing zoo.
3 Nev-er a-gain, No-ah, will God flood all the earth.

Nev-er a-gain, No-ah, will you live in a wa-ter park.
Nev-er a-gain, No-ah, will you sleep with cows that moo.
Nev-er a-gain, No-ah, will you have to hunt for dirt.

For God sent a rain-bow, red, green, yel-low, and blue.

He made a rain-bow just to say his prom-is-es are true.

Words and music: Anita Wagoner; arr. C. Barny Robertson

66 Arky, Arky

1 The Lord told No-ah, there's gon-na be a flood-y, flood-y.
Lord told No-ah, there's gon-na be a flood-y, flood-y.
Get those an-i-mals out of the mud-dy, mud-dy,
chil-dren of the Lord. So rise and shine, and
give God the glo-ry, glo-ry. Rise and shine, and

Words and music: traditional; arr. Joyce Borger
Arr. © 2006, Faith Alive Christian Resources

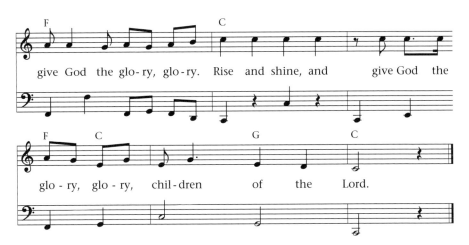

give God the glo - ry, glo - ry. Rise and shine, and give God the

glo - ry, glo - ry, chil - dren of the Lord.

Additional stanzas:

2 The Lord told Noah to build him an arky, arky.
  Lord told Noah to build him an arky, arky.
  Build it out of gopher barky, barky,
  children of the Lord.
  Refrain

3 The animals, the animals, they came in by twosies, twosies.
  Animals, the animals, they came in by twosies, twosies,
  elephants and kangaroosies, roosies,
  children of the Lord.
  Refrain

4 It rained and poured for forty daysies, daysies.
  Rained and poured for forty daysies, daysies.
  Almost drove those animals crazies, crazies,
  children of the Lord.
  Refrain

5 The sun came out and dried up the landy, landy.
  (Look, there's the sun!) It dried up the landy, landy.
  Everything was fine and dandy, dandy,
  children of the Lord.
  Refrain

Who Built the Ark

Words and music: traditional American; adapted by Patricia Nederveld; arr. Emily R. Brink, 1992

Father Abraham 68

Capo 1

1 Father Abraham had many kids, many kids had Father Abraham. I am one of them, and so are you, so let's all praise the Lord. *Right arm!

Add motions: Right arm! (clench fist, bend and extend right arm upward repeatedly throughout song)

Repeat song, adding motions as follows:

2 Father Abraham had many kids, many kids had Father Abraham. I am one of them and so are you, so let's all praise the Lord.
   left arm! (add left arm in same motion as right)

3 . . . *right foot! (add right foot stepping up and down)*

4 . . . *left foot! (add left foot stepping up and down)*

5 . . . *chin up! (start a continuous chin-bobbing motion)*

6 . . . *turn around! (add turning in place while continuing other motions)*

7 . . . *sit down! (sit down)*

Words and music: traditional; arr. Joyce Borger
Arr. © 2006, Faith Alive Christian Resources

69 Yahweh Is Calling

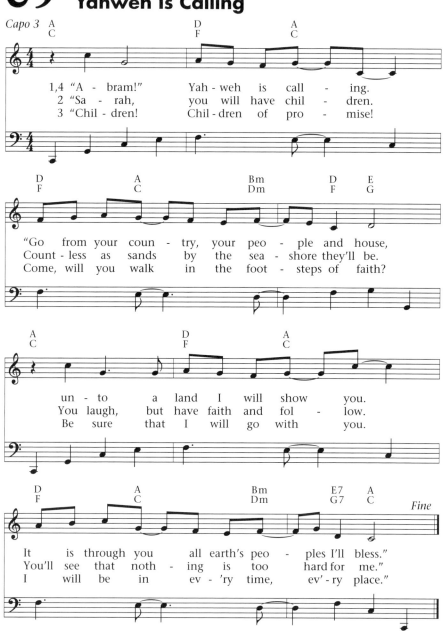

Capo 3

1,4 "A - bram!" Yah - weh is call - ing.
2 "Sa - rah, you will have chil - dren.
3 "Chil - dren! Chil - dren of pro - mise!

"Go from your coun - try, your peo - ple and house,
Count - less as sands by the sea - shore they'll be.
Come, will you walk in the foot - steps of faith?

un - to a land I will show you.
You laugh, but have faith and fol - low.
Be sure that I will go with you.

It is through you all earth's peo - ples I'll bless."
You'll see that noth - ing is too hard for me."
I will be in ev - 'ry time, ev' - ry place."

Words and music: Susan Mulder Langeland

JACQUI'S SONG

70 Song of Joseph

Capo 3

1 Young Joseph's father liked him best, which
2 But God watched over Joseph there, and
3 But then a famine struck the earth, and
4 God had a plan to save his own, the
5 God can turn evil into good, and

made his brothers mad. They sent him off to
with his powerful hand he caused the crops to
all the fields were dry. All Joseph's brothers
people that he loved. Now Joseph's family
right he makes from wrong. O praise his name for -

E-gypt-land, so lonely and so sad.
fill the fields. Now Joseph ruled the land.
came to him for food that they could buy.
joined him there and praised our God above.
evermore and fill each day with song.

Words: Bonnie Bratt Meyer, 1983; alt.
Music: Emily R. Brink, 1994
© 1983, 1994, CRC Publications

When Israel Was in Egypt's Land

1 When Is-rael was in E-gypt's land, op-
2 The Lord told Mo-ses what to do, Let my peo-ple go, to
3 As Is-rael stood by the wa-ter-side, at

pressed so hard they could not stand,
lead the He-brew chil-dren through, Let my peo-ple go.
God's com-mand it did di-vide,

Refrain

Go down, Mo-ses, way down in E-gypt's land,

tell old Pha-raoh: Let my peo-ple go.

Accompaniment for Orff or other C instrument

Words and music: African-American spiritual; arr. Emily R. Brink, 1993
Arr. © 1994, CRC Publications

GO DOWN, MOSES

72 God's Story

Refrain

It's God's stor-y; you know it's true. It's God's

stor-y, 'cause he loves you. It's God's

4th time to Coda

stor-y; you know it's true. It's God's

stor-y, 'cause he loves you. 1 God

cared for ba-by Mo-ses float-ing on the Nile.
2 Through the frogs and bugs and hail God was true.
3 Stand-ing at the Red Sea, Mo-ses raised his hand. Then

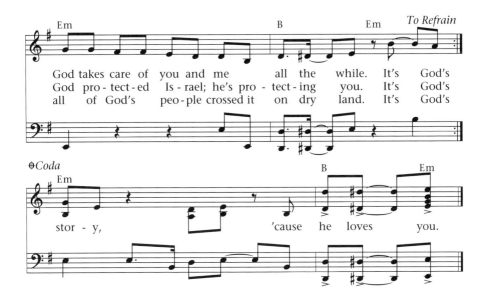

God takes care of you and me all the while. It's God's
God pro-tect-ed Is-rael; he's pro-tect-ing you. It's God's
all of God's peo-ple crossed it on dry land. It's God's

Coda

stor - y, 'cause he loves you.

73 How Did Moses Cross the Red Sea

How did Mo-ses cross the Red Sea? How did Mo-ses cross the Red Sea? How did Mo - ses cross the Red Sea? How did he get a - cross? Did he swim? No, no. Did he sail? No, no. Did he fly? No, no, no, no. Did he walk? No, no. Did he run? No, no. How did he get a -

Words and music: Hugh Mitchell

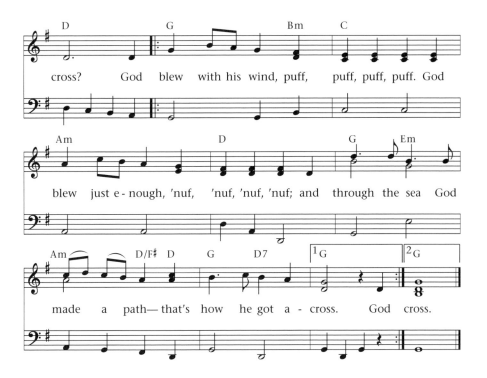

cross?   God   blew   with his wind, puff,   puff, puff, puff. God

blew   just e - nough, 'nuf,   'nuf, 'nuf, 'nuf; and   through the sea   God

made   a   path—that's how   he got a - cross.   God   cross.

74 Be Bold, Be Strong

Words and music: Morris Chapman

75 Joshua Fought the Battle of Jericho

Words and music: African-American spiritual; arr. Emily R. Brink, 1992
Arr. © 1994, CRC Publications

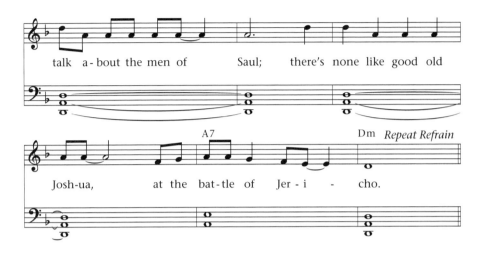

talk a-bout the men of Saul; there's none like good old

A7   Dm   *Repeat Refrain*

Josh-ua, at the bat-tle of Jer - i - cho.

2 Up to the walls of Jericho
   he marched with sword in hand.
   "Go blow those ram's horns," Joshua cried,
   "for the battle is in God's hands." *Refrain*

3 Then the horns began to bellow,
   the trumpets began to sound,
   and Joshua commanded the children to shout,
   and the walls came tumbling down. *Refrain*

76 Only a Boy Named David

Capo 3

On-ly a boy named Da-vid, on-ly a lit-tle sling, on-ly a boy named Da-vid, but he could pray and sing. On-ly a boy named Da-vid, on-ly a rip-pling brook, on-ly a boy named Da-vid, but five lit-tle stones he took. And one lit-tle stone went in the sling, and the sling went round and

Words and music: Arthus Arnott, 1931; based on 1 Samuel 17:49

round. And one lit-tle stone went in the sling, and the sling went round and round, and round and round and round and round, and round and round and round. And one lit-tle stone went up in the air, and the giant came tum-bling down.

Motions:

(a) *Hand held out, palm down, as if measuring.*
(b) *Circle hand above head.*
(c) *Hands folded.*
(d) *Wiggle fingers, moving arm left to right.*
(e) *Hold up five fingers.*
(f) *Hold up one finger.*
(g) *Shoot arm forward.*
(h) *Fall down or clap.*

77 Jonah's Song

1 In my trou - ble, in my trou - ble I
2 I was sink - ing, I was sink - ing in
3 Those who wor - ship worth - less i - dols will

cried out to the Lord, my God, and,
dark - ness to the o - cean floor, and,
nev - er know the grace of God, but,

Lord, you heard me; yes, you heard me;

from the depths you heard my cry.

Though the wa - ter swirled a - round me,
When my prayer came to your tem - ple,
With a song of high thanks - giv - ing

Words: Edith Bajema
Music: Vicki Williams, 1994
© 1994, CRC Publications

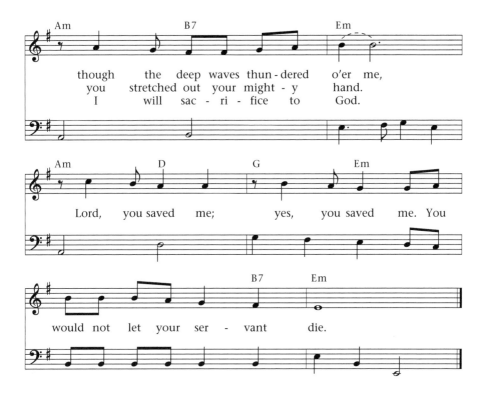

though   the   deep   waves   thun - dered   o'er   me,
you   stretched   out   your   might - y   hand.
I   will   sac - ri - fice   to   God.

Lord,   you   saved   me;   yes,   you   saved   me.   You

would   not   let   your   ser - vant   die.

Who Did Swallow Jonah

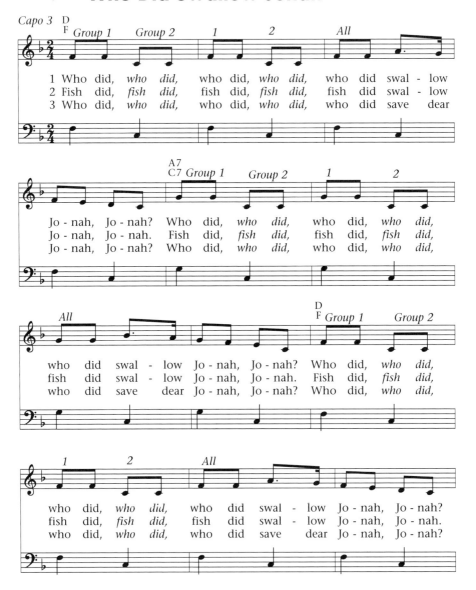

Capo 3

1 Who did, *who did,* who did, *who did,* who did swal-low Jo-nah, Jo-nah? Who did, *who did,* who did, *who did,* who did swal-low Jo-nah, Jo-nah? Who did, *who did,* who did, *who did,* who did swal-low Jo-nah, Jo-nah?

2 Fish did, *fish did,* fish did, *fish did,* fish did swal-low Jo-nah, Jo-nah. Fish did, *fish did,* fish did, *fish did,* fish did swal-low Jo-nah, Jo-nah. Fish did, *fish did,* fish did, *fish did,* fish did swal-low Jo-nah, Jo-nah.

3 Who did, *who did,* who did, *who did,* who did save dear Jo-nah, Jo-nah? Who did, *who did,* who did, *who did,* who did save dear Jo-nah, Jo-nah? Who did, *who did,* who did, *who did,* who did save dear Jo-nah, Jo-nah?

Words and music: Pamela Conn Beall and Susan Hagen Nipp, *Wee Sing Bible Songs,* alt.; arr. Joyce Borger
© 1986, Pamela Conn Beall and Susan Hagen Nipp. Reprinted by permission of Price/Stern/Sloan
Publishers, Inc., a division of Penguin Putnam, Inc. Arr. © 2006, Faith Alive Christian Resources.

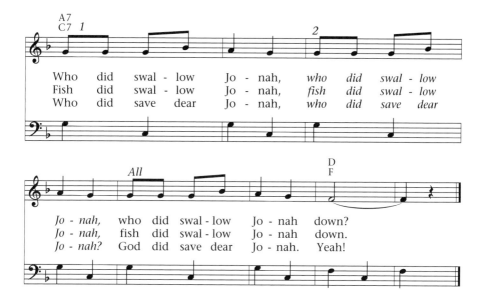

Who did swal - low Jo - nah, who did swal - low
Fish did swal - low Jo - nah, fish did swal - low
Who did save dear Jo - nah, who did save dear

Jo - nah, who did swal - low Jo - nah down?
Jo - nah, fish did swal - low Jo - nah down.
Jo - nah? God did save dear Jo - nah. Yeah!

79 Shadrach, Meshach, and Abednego

Capo 3

Three good men lived ver-y long a-go,
Shad-rach, Me-shach, and A-bed-ne-go.
To an i-dol they would nev-er bow,
Shad-rach, Me-shach, and A-bed-ne-go.
In-to a fi-ery fur-nace they were quick-ly cast,

Ne - bu - chad - nez - zar thought they'd nev - er last. But

God was there; he nev - er let them go—

Shad - rach, Me - shach, and A - bed - ne - go.

80 His Name Will Be John

*Or another name

Words and music: Robert C. Evans

Additional parts for "O Come, O Come, Immanuel"

Duet accompaniment or bells (right hand only)
or alternative accompaniment (both hands)

O Come, O Come, Immanuel

81

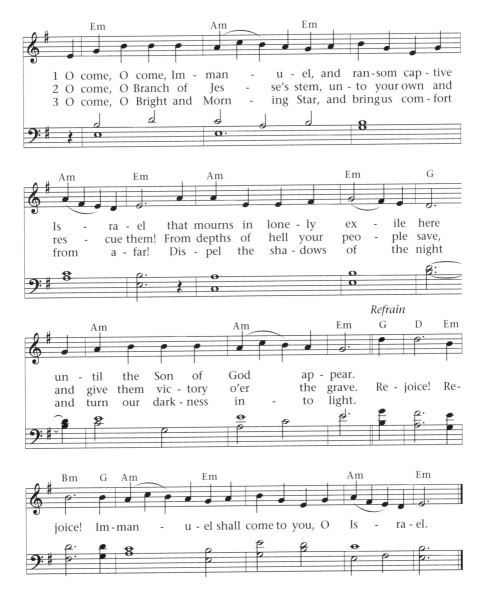

1 O come, O come, Im - man - u - el, and ran-som cap - tive
2 O come, O Branch of Jes - se's stem, un - to your own and
3 O come, O Bright and Morn - ing Star, and bring us com - fort

Is - ra - el that mourns in lone - ly ex - ile here
res - cue them! From depths of hell your peo - ple save,
from a - far! Dis - pel the sha - dows of the night

Refrain

un - til the Son of God ap - pear. Re - joice! Re -
and give them vic - tory o'er the grave.
and turn our dark - ness in - to light.

joice! Im-man - u - el shall come to you, O Is - ra - el.

Words: Latin, 12th century; composite translation
Music: *Processionale*, 15th century; adapted by Thomas Helmore, 1854;
   arr. Richard Proulx, 1975; adapted by Robert Roth, 1989
Accompaniment © 1975, GIA Publications, Inc. Used by permission.

LM
VENI IMMANUEL

82 Magnify the Lord

Words: Bert Polman, 1985; based on the Song of Mary, Luke 1:46-49
Music: Jacques Berthier, 1984

MAGNIFICAT

who has done great things for me.

4
C   D7   G
mag - ni - fy the Lord who is my Sav - ior!

83 Come, Thou Long-Expected Jesus

Capo 3

1 Come, thou long-ex-pec-ted Je-sus, born to set thy
2 Is - rael's strength and con-so - la - tion, hope of all the
3 Born thy peo-ple to de-liv-er, born a child and
4 By thine own e - ter-nal Spir-it rule in all our

peo - ple free; from our fears and sins re - lease us,
earth thou art: dear de - sire of ev - ery na - tion,
yet a king, born to reign in us for - ev - er,
hearts a - lone; by thine all - suf - fi - cient mer - it

let us find our rest in thee.
joy of ev - ery long - ing heart.
now thy gra - cious king - dom bring.
raise us to thy glo - rious throne.

Words: Charles Wesley, 1744
Music: *Psalmodia Sacra*, 1715; adapted by Henry Gauntlett, 1861; arr. Robert Roth, 1989
Arr. © 1989, Robert Roth. Used by permission.

87 87
STUTTGART

Prepare the Way of the Lord

84

Pre - pare the way of the Lord. Pre-pare the way of the Lord,

and all peo-ple will see the sal - va - tion of our God.

Varied accompaniments and solos
Recorder (alto) or Flute

Bass xylophone   *Alto metalaphone*   *Soprano glockenspiel*

Piano accompaniment

For a piano duet, one person
plays the melody an octave higher
while the other person plays this
pattern four times.

Words: Isaiah 40:3; 52:10
Music: Jacques Berthier and the Community of Taizé, 1984

85 People in Darkness Are Looking for Light

1 Peo - ple in dark - ness are look-ing for light.
2 Peo - ple with sick - ness are pray-ing for health.
3 Peo - ple in trou - ble would like to be free.
4 Peo - ple in sad - ness are yearn-ing to sing.

Come, come, come, Je - sus Christ.
Come, come, come, Je - sus Christ.
Come, come, come, Je - sus Christ.
Come, come, come, Je - sus Christ.

Peo - ple with blind-ness are long - ing for sight.
Peo - ple in pov - er - ty want to have wealth.
Peo - ple with ar - gu - ments want to a - gree.
Peo - ple in grief want re - lief from death's sting.

Come, Lord Je - sus Christ. These
Come, Lord Je - sus Christ. These
Come, Lord Je - sus Christ. These
Come, Lord Je - sus Christ. These

Words and music: Dosia Carlson, 1983
© 1986, 1997, Dosia Carlson. Used by permission.

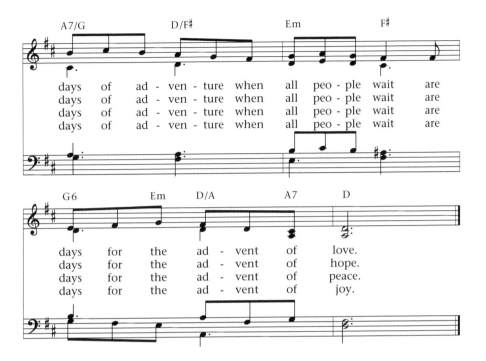

days of ad - ven - ture when all peo - ple wait are
days of ad - ven - ture when all peo - ple wait are
days of ad - ven - ture when all peo - ple wait are
days of ad - ven - ture when all peo - ple wait are

days for the ad - vent of love.
days for the ad - vent of hope.
days for the ad - vent of peace.
days for the ad - vent of joy.

86 Make Way

1 Make way, make way, for Christ the King in splen-dor ar-rives.
2 He comes the bro-ken hearts to heal, the pris-oners to free.
3 And those who mourn with heav-y hearts, who weep and sigh;
4 We call you now to wor-ship him as Lord of all,

Fling wide the gates and wel-come him in-to your lives.
The deaf shall hear, the lame shall dance, the blind shall see.
with laugh-ter, joy, and roy-al crown he'll beau-ti-fy.
to have no gods be-fore him—their thrones must fall.

Refrain

Make way, *(Make way!)* make way *(Make way)* for the

King of kings. *(for the King of kings.)* Make way, *(Make way!)* make

way! *(Make way!)* And let his king-dom in.

Away in a Manger 87

Capo 3

1 A - way in a man-ger, no crib for a bed,
2 The cat - tle are low - ing, the ba - by a - wakes,
3 Be near me, Lord Je - sus; I ask you to stay

the lit - tle Lord Je - sus laid down his sweet head;
but lit - tle Lord Je - sus, no cry - ing he makes.
close by me for - ev - er and love me, I pray.

the stars in the bright sky looked down where he lay;
I love you, Lord Je - sus: look down from on high
Bless all the dear chil - dren in your ten - der care;

the lit - tle Lord Je - sus a - sleep on the hay.
and stay by my side un - til morn - ing is nigh.
pre - pare us for heav - en to live with you there.

Words: American, 1885
Music: James R. Murray, 1887

11 11 11 11
AWAY IN A MANGER

88 Amen

Words and music: Afro-American spiritual; arr. Greg Scheer, © 2006

Irregular
AMEN

What Can I Give Him

Words: Christina G. Rossetti, 1872; from "In the Bleak Midwinter"
Music: Gustav Holst, 1906

90 Angels We Have Heard on High

Capo 3

1 An - gels we have heard on high, sing - ing sweet-ly through the night,
2 Shep-herds, why this ju - bi - lee? Why these songs of hap - py cheer?
3 Come to Beth - le - hem and see him whose birth the an - gels sing;

and the moun-tains in re - ply, ech - o - ing their brave de-light.
What great bright-ness did you see? What glad tid - ings did you hear?
come, a - dore on bend - ed knee Christ the Lord, the new-born King.

Refrain

Glo - - ri - a

in ex - cel - sis De - o. Glo - -

ri - a in ex - cel - sis De - o.

Words and music: French carol, tr. James Chadwick

77 77 with refrain
GLORIA

He Came Down

1 He came down that we may have hope;* he came down that we may have hope;* he came down that we may have hope.* Hal-le-lu-jah for-ev-er-more. *(Why did he come?)*

*2 joy 3 peace 4 life 5 light

Words and music: Cameroon traditional; arr. John L. Bell

92 Come On, Ring Those Bells

1 Ev - ery - bod - y likes to take a hol - i - day;
2 Cel - e - bra - tions come be - cause of some-thing good,

ev - ery - bod - y likes to take a rest,
cel - e - bra - tions we love to re - call.

spend-ing time to-geth - er with the fam - i - ly,
Mar - y had a ba - by boy in Beth - le-hem, the

shar - ing lots of love and hap - pi - ness.
great - est cel - e - bra - tion of them all.

93 Gloria, Gloria

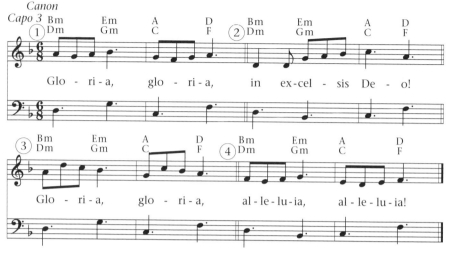

Canon

Glo - ri - a, glo - ri - a, in ex - cel - sis De - o!

Glo - ri - a, glo - ri - a, al - le - lu - ia, al - le - lu - ia!

*For a piano duet, one person plays
only the melody while another person
plays this pattern four times:*

*Orff instrument patterns may be created by repeating any of the four patterns of
the melody or accompaniment.*

Flute descants

Joy to the World 94

1 Joy to the world! The Lord is come: let earth re-
2 Joy to the earth! The Sav-ior reigns: let all their
3 No more let sin and sor-row grow nor thorns in-
4 He rules the world with truth and grace, and makes the

ceive her King. Let ev-ery heart pre-pare him room,
songs em-ploy, while fields and floods, rocks, hills, and plains
fest the ground; he comes to make his bless-ings flow
na-tions prove the glo-ries of his right-eous-ness

and heaven and na-ture sing, and heaven and na-ture
re-peat the sound-ing joy, re-peat the sound-ing
far as the curse is found, far as the curse is
and won-ders of his love, and won-ders of his

and heaven and na-ture sing, and

sing, and heaven, and heaven and na-ture sing.
joy, re-peat, re-peat the sound-ing joy.
found, far as, far as the curse is found.
love, and won-ders, won-ders of his love.

heaven and na-ture sing,

Words: Isaac Watts, 1719; based on Psalm 98
Music: Lowell Mason, 1848

CM with repeats
ANTIOCH

95 Glory to God

Words and music: Keith Currie
© 1991, Integrity Music, Inc. (ASCAP) Used by permission.

a Sav - ior is born.

you   a Sav - ior is born.

Glory to God in the Highest 96

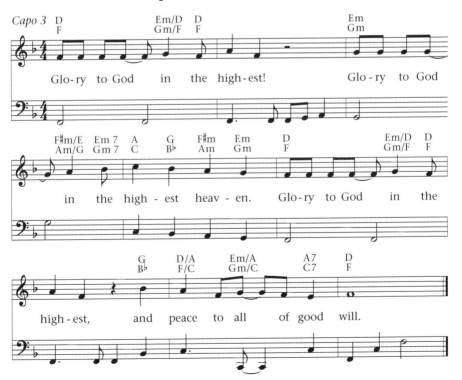

Glo - ry to God   in   the high-est!   Glo - ry to God

in   the high - est heav - en.   Glo - ry to God   in   the

high - est,   and   peace   to   all   of   good   will.

Words and music: Joanne Barrett and Ron E. Long

97 Little Bitty Baby

Mary Had a Baby 98

Capo 3

1 Mar - y had a ba - by. Yes, Lord!
2 What did she name him? Yes, Lord!
3 She named the ba - by Je - sus. Yes, Lord!
4 Where was he born? Yes, Lord!
5 Born in a man - ger. Yes, Lord!

Mar - y had a ba - by. Yes, my Lord!
What did she name him? Yes, my Lord!
She named the ba - by Je - sus. Yes, my Lord!
Where was he born? Yes, my Lord!
Born in a man - ger. Yes, my Lord!

Mar - y had a ba - by. Yes, Lord!
What did she name him? Yes, Lord!
She named the ba - by Je - sus. Yes, Lord!
Where was he born? Yes, Lord!
Born in a man - ger. Yes, Lord!

The lit - tle child of Beth - le - hem was born for us.

Words and music: spiritual

99 Jubilate Deo/Raise a Song of Gladness

Words: Taizé Community, 1978; based on Psalm 100
Music: Jacques Berthier
Music © 1979, Ateliers et Presses de Taizé, Taizé Community, France. GIA Publications, Inc., exclusive North American agent. All rights reserved. Used by permission.

That Boy-Child of Mary 100

That boy-child of Mary was born in a stable, a manger his cradle in Bethlehem.

1 What shall we call him, child of the manger?
His name is Jesu, God ever with us,
He came to save us, he came to help us,

What name is given in Bethlehem?
God given for us in Bethlehem.
born here among us in Bethlehem.

Repeat refrain

4 One with the Father, he is our Savior,
heaven-sent helper of Bethlehem. *Refrain*

5 Gladly we praise him, love and adore him,
give ourselves to him of Bethlehem. *Refrain*

Words: Tom Colvin
Music: traditional Malawi; adapted by Tom Colvin; arr. Norma de Waal Malefyt

101 Mary's Boy Child

1 Long time a - go in Beth - le - hem, so the
2 Jo - seph and his wife, Ma - ry, went to
3 shep - herds watched their flocks by night, all

Ho - ly Bi - ble says,
Beth - le - hem that night, and
seat - ed on the ground, an

Ma - ry's boy child, Je - sus Christ, was
found no place to lay their head, not a
an - gel of the Lord came down and glo -

born on Christ - mas day.
sin - gle room was in sight.
ry shone all a - round.

102 O Come, All Ye Faithful

1 O come, all ye faith - ful, joy - ful and tri - um - phant!
O come ye, O come ye to Beth - le - hem!
Come and be - hold him, born the King of an - gels;

Refrain
O come, let us a - dore him, O come, let us a - dore him,
O come, let us a - dore him, Christ the Lord!

Irregular
ADESTE FIDELES

2 God of God, Light of Light eternal,
  lo, he abhors not the virgin's womb;
  Son of the Father, begotten, not created; *Refrain*

3 Sing, choirs of angels, sing in exultation,
  sing, all ye bright hosts of heaven above:
  "Glory to God, all glory in the highest!" *Refrain*

4 Yea, Lord, we greet thee, born this happy morning;
  Jesus, to thee be all glory given;
  Word of the Father, now in flesh appearing; *Refrain*

Song of Simeon 103

1 Lord, bid your ser-vant go in peace; your word is now ful-filled. These eyes have seen sal-va-tion's dawn, this child so long fore-told.

2 This is the Sav-ior of the world, the Gen-tiles' prom-ised light, God's glo-ry dwell-ing in our midst, the joy of Is-ra-el.

Words: *Nunc Dimittis*, paraphrased by James Quinn, S.J., 1969, 1989.
Music: American folk melody; harm. Annabel Morris Buchanan
Words © 1969, James Quinn, S.J.; Selah Publishing Co., Inc., North American agent.
  Used by permission.

CM
LAND OF REST

104 Tell It!

Children

Tell it, tell the good news, tell the good news a-bout Je - sus. Tell it, tell the good news, tell the good news a-bout Je - sus. *Fine*

Leader

1 Christ was born in Beth - le - hem up - on a bed of
2 I can share the hap - py news with ev - 'ry - one I

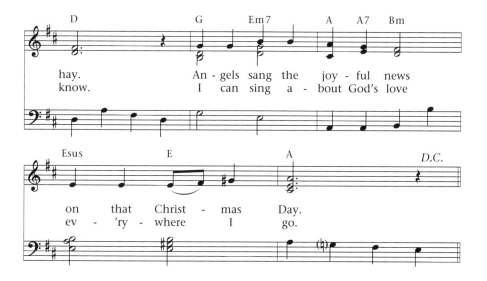

hay.
know.

An - gels sang the joy - ful news
I can sing a - bout God's love

on that Christ - mas Day.
ev - 'ry - where I go.

105 Rock the Baby

Refrain

Rock the ba - by, rock, rock the ba - by, rock the ba - by boy, ba - by Je - sus. Rock the ba - by, rock, rock the ba - by. Rock, rock, Je - sus is born.

1 Christ - mas is here. Let's play and sing— rock the ba - by, rock,
2 But the great - est gift on earth— rock the ba - by, rock,
3 Cook - ies and can - dy, treats and toys— rock the ba - by, rock,
4 But the ba - by born in a stall— rock the ba - by, rock,

rock the ba - by— thank - ing the Lord for ev - ery - thing.
rock the ba - by— is the ba - by Je - sus' birth.
rock the ba - by— make lots of smiles for girls and boys.
rock the ba - by— is the great - est gift of all.

Words and music: Jacquelyn and Jon Negus
© 1993, 1999, Momcat Productions, Inc. Used by permission.

Rock, rock, Je-sus is Rock. Rock, Je-sus is Rock,

rock, Je - sus is born.

Praise to the Infant King 106

Words and music: Nan and Dennis Allen

107 Arise, Be Clothed in the Light

Words and music: Lawrence M. Probes, © 1980. Used by permission.

Come and See 108

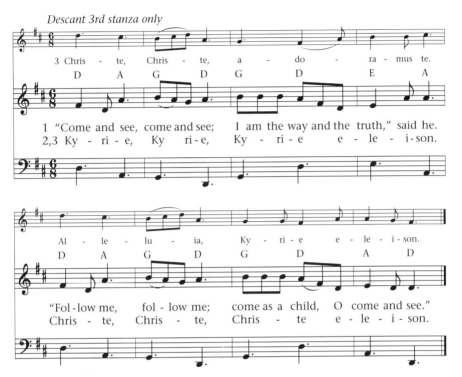

Descant 3rd stanza only

3 Chris - te, Chris - te, a - do - ra - mus te.
D   A   G   D   G   D   E   A

1 "Come and see, come and see; I am the way and the truth," said he.
2,3 Ky - ri - e, Ky ri - e, Ky - ri - e e - le - i - son.

Al - le - lu - ia, Ky - ri - e e - le - i - son.
D   A   G   D   G   D   A   D

"Fol-low me, fol - low me; come as a child, O come and see."
Chris - te, Chris - te, Chris - te e - le - i - son.

Translation:
Stanzas 2-3: Lord, have mercy. Christ, have mercy
Descant: Christ, we adore you. Alleluia, Lord have mercy.

Words and music: based on John 1; Marilyn Houser Hamm, 1974; *Sing and Rejoice*, 1979
© 1974, Marilyn Houser Hamm. Used by permission.

109 Blind Man

1 Blind man stood on the road and he cried.
2 Je - sus stood on the road and re - plied,

Blind man stood on the road and he cried.
Je - sus stood on the road and re - plied,

Blind man stood on the road and he cried say - ing,
Je - sus stood on the road and re - plied, say - ing,

"Ah!_____ Show me the
"Ah!_____ I am the

Words: traditional
Music: traditional; arr. Joyce Borger
Arr. © 2006, Faith Alive Christian Resources

110 Look and Learn

Capo 3

D   D/F♯   G   A
F   F/A   B♭   C

1 Look and learn from the birds of the air, fly - ing
2 Look and learn from the flowers of the field, bring - ing
3 What God wants should be our will; where God

F♯m7 / Am7   Em7 / Gm7   D / F   D/F♯ / F/A

high a - bove wor - ry and fear; nei - ther sow - ing nor
beau - ty and col - or to life; nei - ther sew - ing nor
calls should be our goal. When we seek the

G / B♭   A / C   F♯m7 / Am7   Em7 / Gm7

har - vest - ing seed, yet they're gi - ven what - ev - er they
tai - lor - ing cloth, yet they're dressed in the fin - est at -
king - dom first, all we've lost is ours a -

D / F   A/C♯ / C/E   Bm / Dm   Em7 / Gm7

need. If the God of earth and heaven
tire. If the God of earth and heaven
gain. Let's be done with anx - ious thoughts,

Words and music: Nah Young-Soo, Korean; based on Matthew 6:23-24; tr. and arr. John Bell
Arr. © Wild Goose Resource Group, the Iona Community, Scotland, GIA Publications, Inc., exclusive North American agent. All rights reserved. Used by permission.

cares   for birds   as   much   as this,   won't   he   care   much
cares   for flowers   as   much   as this,   won't   he   care   much
set   a - side   to - mor - row's cares,   live   each   day   that

more   for   you,   when   you put   your   trust   in him?
more   for   you,   when   you put   your   trust   in him?
God   pro - vides,   put - ting all   our   trust   in him.

111 God's Not Dead

God's not dead; (No!) he is a-live. God's not dead; (No!)
he is a-live. God's not dead; (No!) he is a-live. I
know he's liv-ing in me. I see him in my hands, I
see him in my feet, I see him in the air, I
see him ev-'ry-where. I see him at the church, I

see him on   the street,   and   I   know he's   liv-ing in

me. No, no, no, no, no, no, no,   no, no, no, no, no, no, no.

112

I Am the Light of the World

Capo 3

I am the light of the world, I am the
will nev-er walk in the dark, will nev-er

light of the world. Who-ev-er fol-lows me
walk in the dark, but

have the light of life.

Maracas

Words: John 8:12
Music: June Fischer Armstrong, 1991

Peter and James and John

Capo 3

1 Pe - ter and James and John in a sail - boat, *(rocking action, arms cradled)*
Pe - ter and James and John in a sail - boat, *(rocking action)* Pe - ter and James and
John in a sail - boat, *(rocking action)* out on the beau - ti - ful sea.

Additional stanzas:

(casting out, pulling in)   *(hands upturned)*
2   They fished all night, but they caught nothing, *(3x)* . . .

(arms swinging)
3   Along came Jesus walkin' on the seashore, *(3x)* . . .

(two-armed, overhand throw)
4   He said, "Throw your nets over on the other side, *(3x)* . . ."

(spread arms high and wide)
5   The nets were filled with great big fishes, *(3x)* . . .

114

Let the Little Children Come

Words and music: Frank Hernandez

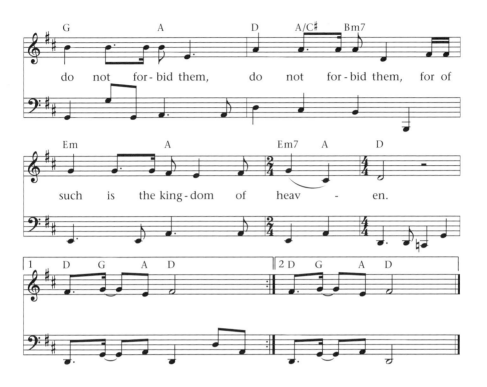

115

Peter's Chanty

1 You ne - ver saw old Ga - li - lee so
2 Out where the sea runs green and cold and
3 And then the clouds grew grim and black; there
4 The rain poured down, the waves leapt high, the

friend - ly and so fair. My mates and I sang
man - y fath - oms deep, I called my mates, "Look
blew an aw - ful gale. "Heave to, my mates, the
winds they whipped us round and tossed us toward the

mer - ri - ly and ne - ver had a
in the hold! The Mas - ter's gone a -
mast will crack, if we don't low'r the
terri - ble sky and roared their terri - ble

care, and ne - ver had a care.
sleep! The Mas - ter's gone a - sleep!"
sail, if we don't low'r the sail!"
sound, and roared their terri - ble sound.

Words: Herman G. Stuempfle, Jr.
Music: Ben DeVan

86866
PETER'S CHANTY

5 We roused the Master from his sleep
  and called his name in dread:
  "Come, save us from the awful deep,
  or we're as good as dead,
  or we're as good as dead!"

6 Then up he stood against the gale,
  and told the storm to cease.
  Tempestuous winds broke off their wail;
  waves calmed and lay at peace,
  waves calmed and lay at peace.

7 So, friends, although the sea be wide,
  and though your boat be small,
  there's naught to fear from time or tide;
  the Master's Lord of all,
  the Master's Lord of all.

8 Then sing, my friends, sing merrily;
  O sing both bold and brave.
  The One who made the surging sea
  still rules the wind and wave,
  still rules the wind and wave.

116 The Good Samaritan

1 A cer-tain travel-er on his way was robbed and left to die. Help-less by the road he lay, and no one heard his cry. A cer-tain priest came down that way, a man most dig-ni - fied. "I will not get in-volved," said he and passed on the oth - er

2 A cer-tain Le - vite came that way, a man of wealth and pride. "I'm much too bus-y to stop," said he and passed on the oth-er side. But a cer-tain man from Sa-mar - i - a, a strang-er in the land, took pi - ty on the in - jured man and lent a help-ing

Words and music: Mary Lu Walker; arr. H. Myron Braun
© 1998, Mary Lu Walker. From the collection *Dandelions* (Paulist Press, 1975).

side.
Don't pass your neigh-bor by, my friend; don't
hand.

pass your neigh - bor by. Love your neigh - bor

as your - self; don't pass your neigh - bor by.

117

The Sower

1 A farm-er went out to plant the seed. The
2 And some of the seed fell on the rocks. The
3 And some of the seed fell on good soil. The

sow-er went out to sow. And some of the seed the
sow-er went out to sow. And some of the seed fell
sow-er went out to sow. The seed that was sown there

birds ate up. The sow-er went out to sow.
in the thorns. The sow-er went out to sow.
bore much fruit. The sow-er went out to sow.

Refrain

God's Word is the good seed that

Words and music: Kathleen Hart Brumm
© 1988, 1995, Brummhart Publishing Company

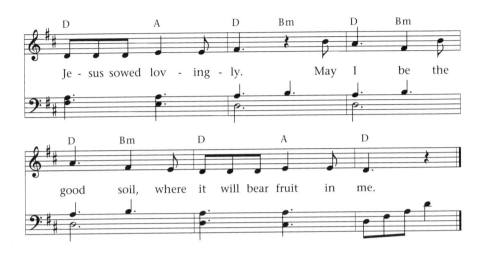

Je - sus sowed lov - ing - ly. May I be the good soil, where it will bear fruit in me.

118 The Wise Man and the Foolish Man

Capo 3

1 The wise man built his house up-on the rock. The
2 The fool-ish man built his house up-on the sand. The

wise man built his house up-on the rock. The
fool-ish man built his house up-on the sand. The

wise man built his house up-on the rock. And the
fool-ish man built his house up-on the sand. And the

rains came tum-bling down. The rains came down, and the

floods came up. The rains came down, and the floods came up.

Words: adapted from Matthew 7:24-27
Music: unknown

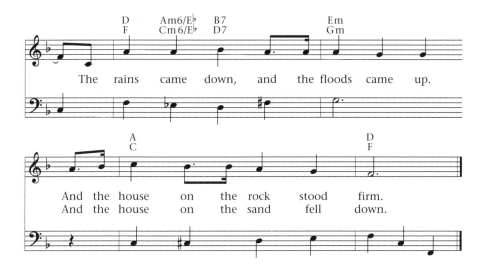

The rains came down, and the floods came up.

And the house on the rock stood firm.
And the house on the sand fell down.

119 This Is My Commandment

Capo 3
Round

This is my com-mand-ment, that you love one an-

oth- er that your joy may be full. *Fine*

This is my com-mand-ment, that you love one an-

oth- er that your joy may be full, that your

joy may be full, that your joy may be full. *D.C. al Fine*

Additional stanzas:

This is my commandment, that you trust one another . . .
. . . serve one another . . .
. . . lay down your lives . . .

Words: John 15:11-12
Music: anonymous; arr. Richard L. Van Oss, 1992
Arr. © 1994, CRC Publications

When Jesus the Healer 120

1 When Jesus the heal-er passed through Gal-i-lee,
2 A par-a-lyzed man was let down through a roof.
3 The death of his daugh-ter caused Jai-rus to weep.
4 When blind Bar-ti-mae-us cried out to the Lord,

Heal us, heal us to-day!

the deaf came to hear and the blind came to see.
His sins were for-giv-en, his walk-ing the proof.
The Lord took her hand, and he raised her from sleep.
his faith made him whole and his sight was re-stored.

Heal us, Lord Je-sus!

5 The lepers were healed and the demons cast out. Heal us, heal us today!
A bent woman straightened to laugh and to shout. Heal us, Lord Jesus.

6 The twelve were commissioned and sent out in twos. Heal us, heal us today!
To make the sick whole and to spread the good news. Heal us, Lord Jesus.

7 There's still so much sickness and suffering today. Heal us, heal us today!
We gather together for healing and pray: Heal us, Lord Jesus.

Words and music: Peter D. Smith

11 6 11 5
HEALER

121 Zacchaeus

Capo 3

1 Zac - chae - us was a wee lit - tle man, a wee lit - tle man was he. He climbed up in a syc - a-more tree, for the Lord he wanted to see. And as the Sav - ior passed that way, he looked up in the tree, *and he said,* for I'm go - ing to your house to -
"Zaccheus, you come down,

(Spoken)

Words: st. 1, traditional; st. 2, Herman Proper, 1980
Music: traditional; arr. N. R. Schaper
St. 2 © 1994, CRC Publications.

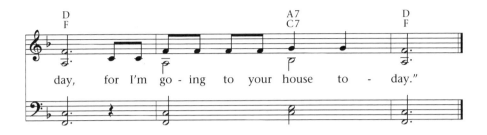

day,   for I'm go - ing to your house   to - day."

2 Zacchaeus knew that he'd done wrong,
   and sorry for his sins was he.
   "Lord, to the poor I'll give one half
   of all my goods," said he.
   "And if I've cheated anyone,
   four times will I repay."
      And Jesus said,
      "Salvation has come to you!
   I have come to seek and save.
   I have come to seek and save."

122 Lamb of Glory

Words and music: Greg Nelson and Phill McHugh

Oh, How He Loves You and Me

123

1 Oh, how he loves you and me.
2 Je - sus to Cal - vary did go,

Oh, how he loves you and me.
love for all peo - ple to show;

He gave his life— what more could he give?
what he did there brought hope from de - spair.

Refrain

Oh, how he loves you; oh, how he loves me;

oh, how he loves you and me!

Words and music: Kurt Kaiser

124 Lamb of God

Words: based on 1 Peter 1:18-19
Music: Twila Paris

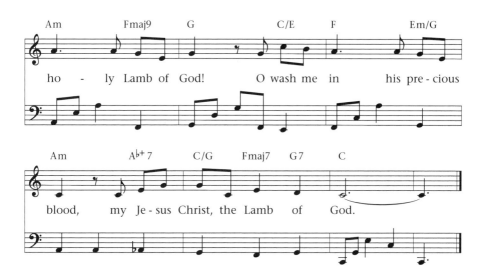

ho - ly Lamb of God! O wash me in his pre - cious blood, my Je - sus Christ, the Lamb of God.

125 Shout Hosanna

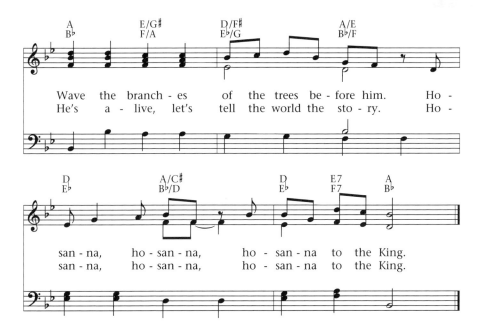

Wave the branch - es of the trees be - fore him. Ho -
He's a - live, let's tell the world the sto - ry. Ho -

san - na, ho - san - na, ho - san - na to the King.
san - na, ho - san - na, ho - san - na to the King.

126 We Have a King

Refrain

and his name is Je - sus.
for the King called Je - sus.
and his name is Je - sus. Je - sus the
Ser - vant King is Je - sus.
Give it up in ser - vice!

King is ris - en, Je - sus the King is ris - en,

Je - sus the King is ris - en ear - ly in the morn - ing.

127 This Is How We Know

Words: 1 John 3:16 (NIV)
Music: Frank Hernandez, 1990; arr. Norma de Waal Malefyt, 1992

128 There Is a Redeemer

1 There is a Re-deem-er, Je-sus, God's own Son;
2 Je-sus, my Re-deem-er, name a-bove all names,
3 When I stand in glo-ry I will see his face;

pre-cious Lamb of God, Mes-si-ah, Ho - ly One.
pre-cious Lamb of God, Mes-si-ah, hope for sin-ners slain.
there I'll serve my King for-ev-er, in that ho-ly place.

Refrain

Thank you, O my Fa-ther, for giv-ing us your Son, and

leav - ing your Spir-it till the work on earth is done.

Words and music: Melody Green

Alleluia, Alleluia, Give Thanks

129

Capo 3

Refrain

Al - le - lu - ia, al - le - lu - ia! Give thanks to the ris - en Lord.

Al - le - lu - ia, al - le - lu - ia! Give praise to his name.

Fine

1 Je - sus is Lord of all the earth;
2 Spread the good news o'er all the earth:
3 We have been cru - ci - fied with Christ;
4 Come, let us praise the liv - ing God,

he is the King of cre - a - tion.
Je - sus has died and has ris - en.
now we shall live for - ev - er.
joy - ful - ly sing to our Sav - ior.

D.C.

130 Alive, Alive

A - live, a - live, a - live for-ev-er-more! My

Je - sus is a - live, a - live for-ev-er-more! A -

live, a - live, a - live for-ev-er-more! My

Je - sus is a - live. Sing hal-le-lu-jah!

Sing hal-le-lu-jah! My Je - sus is a -

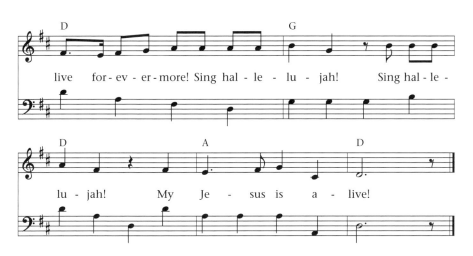

live for - ev - er - more! Sing hal - le - lu - jah! Sing hal - le - lu - jah! My Je - sus is a - live!

He's Alive 131

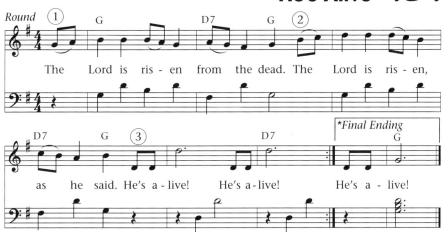

Round ① G   D7   G ②

The Lord is ris - en from the dead. The Lord is ris - en,

D7   G ③   D7   *Final Ending* G

as he said. He's a - live! He's a - live! He's a - live!

*After group ③ is finished, everyone sings the final ending together.

Orff or other C instruments
Bass xylophone   *Alto xylophone*

Alto glockenspiel   *Soprano glockenspiel*

132 Christ the Lord Is Risen Today

1 Christ the Lord is risen to-day! Al - le - lu - ia!
2 Love's re-deem-ing work is done, Al - le - lu - ia!
3 Lives a-gain our glo-rious King; Al - le - lu - ia!

All cre-a-tion, join to say: Al - le - lu - ia!
Fought the fight, the bat-tle won; Al - le - lu - ia!
Where, O death, is now your sting? Al - le - lu - ia!

Raise your joys and tri-umphs high; Al - le - lu - ia!
Death in vain for-bids him rise; Al - le - lu - ia!
Once he died, our souls to save; Al - le - lu - ia!

Sing, O heavens, and earth, re-ply: Al - le - lu - ia!
Christ has o-pened par-a-dise. Al - le - lu - ia!
Where your vic-to-ry, O grave? Al - le - lu - ia!

Words: Charles Wesley, 1739, alt.
Music: *Lyra Davidica*, 1708; arr. Emily Brink, 1993
Arr. © 1994, CRC Publications

Goodness Is Stronger Than Evil 133

GOODNESS IS STRONGER

134 Halle, Halle, Halle

Solo (sung over hummed refrain)

1 O God, to whom shall we go? You a - lone have the
2 My sheep hear my voice, says the Lord. When I call them, they
4 Now Christ is raised up from death. He will nev - er

words of life. Let your words be our prayer and the
fol - low me. I will lead them to rest by the
die a - gain. All who fol - low his way shall have

song we sing:
peace - ful streams: hal - le - lu - jah, hal - le - lu - jah.
life in him:

3 I am the light of the world, says the Lord. Walk in the

light of life. All who fol - low my words shall have

life in - deed: hal - le - lu - jah, hal - le - lu - jah.

Option 1   Option 2

Congas:

Maracas:

Wood Blocks:

Claves:

135 Mighty Resurrection Day

Words and music: Nancy Gordon

We have been giv - en a might - y res - ur -

rec - tion day!

There was a

136 The Lord Is Risen, Yes, Indeed!

Refrain
Descant for bells or melody instrument

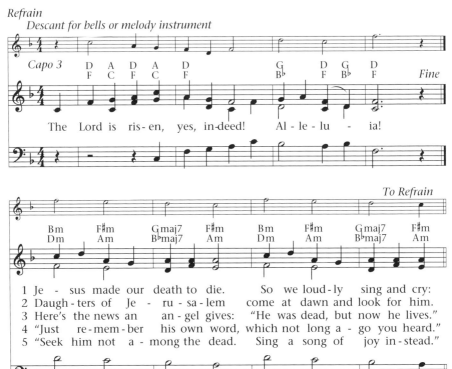

Capo 3

The Lord is ris-en, yes, in-deed! Al - le - lu - ia!

To Refrain

1 Je - sus made our death to die.   So we loud-ly   sing and cry:
2 Daugh-ters of Je - ru - sa-lem   come at dawn and look for him.
3 Here's the news an   an - gel gives: "He was dead, but now he lives."
4 "Just   re-mem-ber   his own word, which not long a - go you heard."
5 "Seek him not a - mong the dead.   Sing a song of   joy in-stead."

Ostinato for Orff or other C instruments

Words: based on Matthew 28:1-6; versified in *Alles wordt nieuw*, 1966, 1971;
    tr. Sietze Buning, 1982
Music: Wim ter Burg, 1971
© 1982, Paideia Press

77 with refrain
OPGESTAAN

Jesus Will Never, Ever

138

He Is Exalted

Words and music: Twila Paris
© 1985, Straightway Music/Mountain Spring Music (admin. EMI Christian Music Publishing).
    All rights reserved. Used by permission.

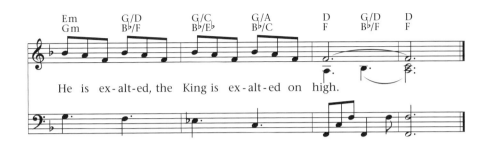

He is ex-alt-ed, the King is ex-alt-ed on high.

He Is the King of Kings 139

Capo 3

He is the King of kings; he is the
Lord of lords. His name is Je-sus, Je-sus,
Je-sus, Je-sus; oh, he is the King.

140 Rejoice, the Lord Is King

1 Re-joice, the Lord is King! Your Lord and King a-dore.
2 His king-dom can-not fail; he rules o'er earth and heaven;
3 He sits at God's right hand till all his foes sub-mit,
4 Re-joice in glo-rious hope; for Christ, the Judge, shall come

Re-joice, give thanks and sing and tri-umph ev-er-more.
the keys of death and hell to Christ the Lord are given.
bow down at his com-mand, and fall be-neath his feet.
to gath-er all his saints to their e-ter-nal home.

Lift up your heart, lift up your voice.
Lift up your heart, lift up your voice.
Lift up your heart, lift up your voice.
We soon shall hear the arch-an-gel's voice;

Re-joice, a-gain I say, re-joice!
Re-joice, a-gain I say, re-joice!
Re-joice, a-gain I say, re-joice!
the trump of God shall sound, re-joice!

Words: Charles Wesley, 1744
Music: John Darwall, 1770; harm. Charlotte Larsen, 1992
Harm. © 1994, CRC Publications

66 66 88
DARWALL'S 148th

The Lord Is a Mighty God

141

Round

The Lord is a might-y God and a might-y King o-ver all the earth. O praise him, O praise him, the King o-ver all the earth. The King o-ver all the earth.

Words: from Psalm 95:3
Music: David Maddux

142 I'm Gonna Sing

I'm gon-na sing* when the Spir-it says sing. I'm gon-na

sing when the Spir-it says sing. I'm gon-na sing when the

Spir-it says sing, and o-bey the Spir-it of the Lord.

*2 pray   3 cry   4 shout

Words and music: African-American spiritual

It Is the Holy Spirit's Day/
To Jesus Christ the Children Sang

143

1 It is the Ho - ly Spir - it's day; sing
2 With rush - ing sound, with heav'n - ly flame on

joy - ful al - le - lu - ia! When all Christ's peo - ple
them the Ho - ly Spir - it came: they blessed and praised God's

met to pray; sing joy - ful al - le - lu - ia!
glo - rious name; sing joy - ful al - le - lu - ia!

Palm Sunday text:

1 To Jesus Christ the children sang,
  Hosanna, Lord! Hosanna!
  Through city streets their voices rang,
  Hosanna, Lord! Hosanna!

2 To Jesus Christ, the children's King,
  Hosanna, Lord! Hosanna!
  With joyful hearts our praise we bring:
  Hosanna, Lord! Hosanna!

Music: traditional Cornish
Words reprinted by permission of St. Christopher's College, London, England.

144 Look What God Is Doing

Words and music: Scott Wesley Brown, Dwight Liles, and Niles Borop

Spirit, Be Our Breath of Life

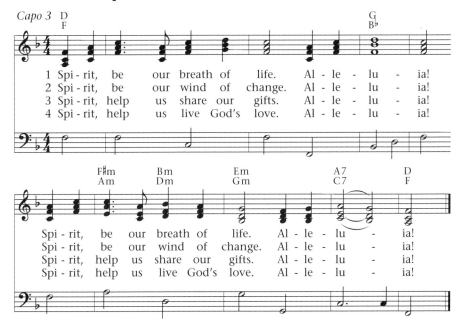

Capo 3

1 Spi - rit, be our breath of life. Al - le - lu - ia!
2 Spi - rit, be our wind of change. Al - le - lu - ia!
3 Spi - rit, help us share our gifts. Al - le - lu - ia!
4 Spi - rit, help us live God's love. Al - le - lu - ia!

Spi - rit, be our breath of life. Al - le - lu - ia!
Spi - rit, be our wind of change. Al - le - lu - ia!
Spi - rit, help us share our gifts. Al - le - lu - ia!
Spi - rit, help us live God's love. Al - le - lu - ia!

Music: traditional ("Michael, Row the Boat Ashore")

146 The Fruit of the Spirit

Capo 3

The fruit of the Spir-it is love, joy, peace, pa-tience, kind-ness, good-ness. The fruit of the Spir-it is

2nd time to Coda

faith-ful-ness, gen-tle-ness, and self-con-trol. Since we live by the Spir-it, let us

Words and music: Frank Hernandez, based on Galatians 5:22-23, 25

147 Silver and Gold Have I None

1 Pe - ter and John went to *(a)*pray; they met a lame
2 "Sil - ver and gold have I *(c)*none, but what I have

man on the way. He asked for alms and
I *(d)*give to you. In the name of *(e)*Je - sus

*(b)*held out his palms, and this is what Pe - ter did
Christ_____ of Naz - a -reth, *(f)*rise up and

say: walk!" 3 He went *(g)*walk - ing and jump - ing and

*(i)*prais - ing God, *(g)*walk - ing and *(h)*jump - ing and

Words and music: anonymous, based on Acts 3:1-8; arr. Betty Pulkingham, 1974

(i) prais - ing God. "In the name of (e)Je - sus

Christ of Naz - a - reth, (f)rise up and walk."

Motions:

(a) *fold hands, as in prayer*
(b) *hold out palms*
(c) *hold out empty hands, shake head*
(d) *extend hand*
(e) *point upward*
(f) *sweep hands upward*
(g) *march (in place)*
(h) *jump up*
(i) *raise arms*

148 Believe in the Lord

Spoken: "What must I do to be saved?"

Be - lieve in the Lord Je - sus Christ. Be - lieve in the Lord Je - sus Christ, and you will be saved, you will be saved. Be - lieve in the Lord Je - sus Christ.

Words: Acts 16:31
Music: Frank Hernandez

Soon and Very Soon 149

Words and music: Andraé Crouch, 1978
Music: adapted by William Farley Smith, 1987

SOON AND VERY SOON

150 How Great Thou Art

Capo 1

1 O Lord my God, when I in awe - some won - der
2 When through the woods and for - est glades I wan - der,
3 But when I think that God, his Son not spar - ing,
4 When Christ shall come, with shout of ac - cla - ma - tion,

con - sid - er all the works thy hand hath made,
I hear the birds sing sweet - ly in the trees;
sent him to die, I scarce can take it in,
and claim his own, what joy shall fill my heart!

I see the stars, I hear the might - y thun - der,
when I look down from loft - y moun - tain gran - deur
that on the cross, my bur - den glad - ly bear - ing
Then I shall bow in hum - ble ad - o - ra - tion

thy power through - out the u - ni - verse dis - played;
and hear the brook and feel the gen - tle breeze;
he bled and died to take a - way my sin;
and there pro - claim, "My God, how great Thou art!"

Words: Carl Boberg, 1885; tr. Stuart K. Hine, 1949
Music: Swedish folk melody; arr. Stuart K. Hine, 1949

11 10 11 10 with refrain
O STORE GUD

151 True Story

Refrain

God put it in the book, *Right there!* in the Bi-ble. He put it in a book, *Right there!* in the Bi-ble. He put it in a book, *Right there!* in the Bi-ble. He gave us a sto-ry and put it in the book.

To spoken stanzas

Words: st. 1, 4-6, Jacquelyn and Jon Negus; st. 2-3, Jessie Schut
Music: Jacquelyn and Jon Negus

1 There's a true story *(echo)*
  about a man in a boat. *(echo)*
  God told old Noah *(etc.)*
  to get ready to float.
  Bring the animals in;
  bring them two by two.
  Bring your family in;
  we'll have a nautical zoo.
  Well, it started to rain
  by God's command.
  There was nothing left;
  the water covered the land.
  When the raining stopped,
  and the floods went away,
  then a rainbow appeared,
  'cause God has something to say. *Refrain*

2 There's a true story *(echo)*
  about a woman and a town. *(echo)*
  The people of Jericho *(etc.)*
  were feeling mighty down.
  "Israelites are coming here.
  Their God is strong; we live in fear."
  Two spies came into the town.
  The king's soldiers tried
  to hunt them down.
  But Rahab said, "I'm on God's side.
  Come quick and on my roof you'll hide."
  Rahab helped the spies escape
  down the walls, not by the gate.
  Rahab, she was not afraid.
  She loved God and she obeyed. *Refrain*

3 There's a true story *(echo)*
  about a man who was sick. *(echo)*
  But his servant knew *(etc.)*
  the power of God was no trick.
  She said, "My God can make you well."
  So Naaman went to Israel.
  The message made him quiver:
  "You must dip in the Jordan River."
  Naaman said, "NO!"
  His servants said "GO!"
  In the river he did dip:
  One, two, three, four, five, and six.
  The seventh time, oh what a joy!
  His skin was like a baby boy's.
  "Praise God," he did say.
  "Lord, I'll love you and obey." *Refrain*

4 There's a true story *(echo)*
  about a fish and a man. *(echo)*
  Now the man named Jonah *(etc.)*
  didn't like God's plan.
  When God said, "Go,"
  Jonah said, "No."
  And the big, big fish,
  it swallowed him whole.
  Well, Jonah learned
  that he had to obey.
  So the fish spit him out,
  and Jonah went God's way.
  Refrain

5 There's a true story *(echo)*
  about the water and wind. *(echo)*
  Jesus needed a rest. *(etc.)*
  He found a boat and got in.
  Now his friends went along,
  and they started to sail.
  But a storm came up;
  his friends started to wail.
  They said, "Jesus, wake up!
  The storm is ready to kill."
  Then Jesus stood up
  and said, "Peace, be still."
  And everything stopped.
  The wind and water obeyed.
  When Jesus is near,
  no need to be afraid. *Refrain*

6 There's a true story *(echo)*
  about some kids and a man. *(echo)*
  Now the man named Jesus *(etc.)*
  was teaching 'cross the land.
  When the moms brought the kids
  Jesus' friends said, "Go 'way.
  Children aren't welcome here;
  Jesus is busy today."
  But Jesus said,
  "Bring the children to me."
  He said, "I love them so much."
  He held them on his knee.
  So remember this:
  If you're sad and blue,
  we are children of his,
  and Jesus loves us too. *Refrain*

152 Amigos De Cristo

153 Create in Me a Clean Heart

Words and music: anonymous, based on Psalm 51:10-12; arr. Joyce Borger
Arr. © 2006, Faith Alive Christian Resources

Perdón, Señor/Forgive Us, Lord 154

Spanish
1 Per - dón, Se - ñor. Por tan - tas in - jus -
2 Per - dón, Se - ñor. Es - ta - mos en pri -

English
1 For - give us, Lord. For all the world's in -
2 For - give us, Lord. We're shack - led by our

ti - cias, Per - dón, Se - ñor. Por tan - ta in - di - fe -
sio - nes, Per - dón, Se - ñor. Es - cla - vos del pe -
jus - tice, for - give us, Lord. For all of our in -
ha - bits, for - give us, Lord. We're chained to dis - o -

ren - cia, Per - dón, Se - ñor.
ca - do, Per - dón, Se - ñor.
dif - ference, for - give us, Lord.
be - dience, for - give us, Lord.

Spanish solista

3 Al perdonar a otros, . . .
  De acuerdo a tu promesa, . . .

4 Libera hoy tu pueblo, . . .
  Que pueda hoy servirte, . . .

English solo or choir

3 As we forgive each other, . . .
  According to your promise, . . .

4 Deliver us from evil, . . .
  For joyful service free us, . . .

4 74 74
CONFESSION

155 John 3:16

John three six-teen says that God so loved the world

he gave his on-ly be-got-ten Son, that who-ev-er be-lieves

in him will nev-er die but have e-ter-nal life.

Just as I Am, Without One Plea 156

Capo 1

1 Just as I am, with-out one plea,
2 Just as I am, and wait-ing not
3 Just as I am, though tossed a-bout
4 Just as I am, thou wilt re-ceive,

but that thy blood was shed for me,
to rid my soul of one dark blot,
with man-y a con-flict, man-y a doubt,
wilt wel-come, par-don, cleanse, re-lieve;

and that thou bidd'st me come to thee,
to thee, whose blood can cleanse each spot,
fight-ings and fears with-in, with-out,
be-cause thy prom-ise I be-lieve,

O Lamb of God, I come, I come.

Words: Charlotte Elliott, 1836
Music: William B. Bradbury 1849

LM
WOODWORTH

157 I've Been Redeemed

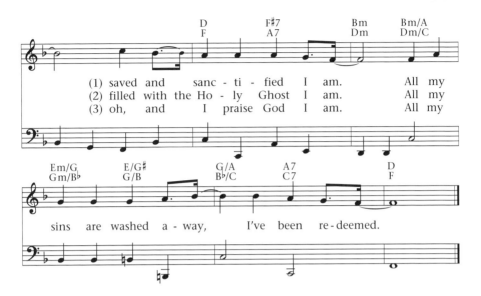

Additional stanzas:

4 And that's not all; *(echo)* there's more besides. *(echo)*
   No, that's not all; *(echo)* there's more besides.
   No, that's not all; there's more besides.
   I've been to the river, and I've been baptized.
   All my sins are washed away, I've been redeemed.

5 He's coming back *(echo)* to take me home. *(echo)*
   He's coming back *(echo)* to take me home. *(echo)*
   He's coming back to take me home.
   I'll shout "Hallelujah" before his throne.
   All my sins are washed away; I've been redeemed.

6 It's by God's grace *(echo)* that I've been saved. *(echo)*
   It's by God's grace *(echo)* that I've been saved.
   It's by God's grace that I've been saved.
   I have no fear on the Judgment Day.
   All my sins are washed away; I've been redeemed.

158 O Christ, the Lamb of God

Capo 3

1, 2 O Christ, the Lamb of God, who takes a - way the
3 O Christ, the Lamb of God, who takes a - way the

sin of the world, have mer - cy up - on us.
sin of the world, grant us your peace.

Final ending

A - men.

Words: *Agnus Dei* (Latin for "Lamb of God"), based on John 1:29
Music: *Kirchenordnung*, Braunschweig, 1528; harm. Dale Grotenhuis, 1984
Harm. © 1987, CRC Publications

CHRISTE, DU LAMM GOTTES

Oh, qué bueno es Jesús/
Oh, How Good Is Christ the Lord

159

English   Oh, how good is Christ the Lord! On the cross he died for me.
Spanish   Oh, qué bue-no es Je-sús. Que por mí mu-rió en la cruz.

He has par-doned all my sin. Glo-ry be to Je-sus.
Mis pe-ca-dos per-do-nó. A su nom-bre glo-ria.

Glo-ry be to Je-sus! Glo-ry be to Je-sus!
A su nom-bre glo-ria. A su nom-bre glo-ria.

In three days he rose a-gain. Glo-ry be to Je-sus.
En tres días re-su-ci-tó. A su nom-bre glo-ria.

Words and music: Puerto Rican folk hymn; harm. Dale Grotenhuis, 1985
Harm. © 1987, CRC Publications

OH QUE BUENO

160

Ask, Seek, Knock

161

Be Thou My Vision

Capo 3

1 Be thou my vi - sion, O Lord of my heart;
2 Be thou my wis - dom, and thou my true word;
3 Rich - es I heed not, nor man's emp - ty praise,
4 High King of heav - en, my vic - to - ry won,

naught be all else to me, save that thou art—
I ev - er with thee and thou with me, Lord;
thou mine in - her - it - ance, now and al - ways;
may I reach heav-en's joys, O bright heav-en's sun!

thou my best thought, by day or by night,
thou my great Fa - ther, I thy true son,
thou and thou on - ly, first in my heart,
Heart of my own heart, what - ev - er be fall,

wak - ing or sleep - ing, thy pres - ence my light.
thou in me dwell - ing, and I with thee one.
high King of heav - en, my treas - ure thou art.
still be my vi - sion, O rul - er of all.

Come and Fill Our Hearts/
Confitemini

162

Ostinato Refrain

English: Come and fill our hearts with your peace.
Latin: Con - fi - te - mi - ni Do - mi - no

You a - lone, O Lord, are ho - ly.
quo - ni - am bo - nus.

Come and fill our hearts with your peace.
Con - fi - te - mi - ni Do - mi - no.

Al - le - lu - ia!
Al - le - lu - ia!

Words: Psalm 136:1 (Latin); Taizé Community, 1982
Music: *Confitemini Domino*, Jacques Berthier

163 Come and Pray in Us

Father in Heaven

164

1 Fa-ther in heav-en, grant to your chil-dren mer-cy and
2 Je-sus, Re-deem-er, may we re-mem-ber your gra-cious
3 Spir-it de-scend-ing, grant us your bless-ing, strength for the

bless-ing, songs nev-er ceas-ing, love to u-nite us, grace to re-
pas-sion, your res-ur-rec-tion; wor-ship we bring you, praise we shall
wea-ry, help for the need-y; sealed by a-dop-tion, we are God's

deem us; Fa-ther in heav-en, Fa-ther, our God.
sing you, Je-sus, Re-deem-er, Je-sus, our Lord.
chil-dren; Spir-it de-scend-ing, Spir-it a-dored.

Words and music: Elena G. Maquiso, 1961; tr. Daniel Thambyrapah Niles, 1964;
   harm. Charles H. Webb, 1987
Translation used by permission of Christian Conference of Asia © 1962, Silliman University Music
   Foundation, Inc.; harm. © 1989, The United Methodist Publishing House (admin. The Copyright Co.).
   All rights reserved. International copyright secured. Used by permission.

165

For Health and Strength

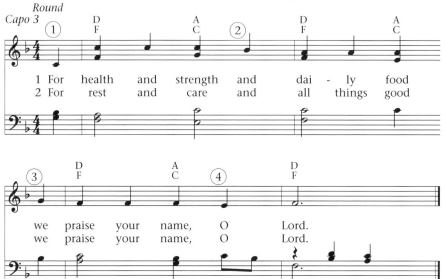

Round
Capo 3

1 For health and strength and dai - ly food
2 For rest and care and all things good

we praise your name, O Lord.
we praise your name, O Lord.

Additional stanzas:

3 For neighbors, friends and family
  we give you thanks, O Lord.

4 For faith and hope and loving care
  we praise your name, O Lord.

Words: st. 1, traditional; st. 2-3, Bert Polman, 1991
Music: traditional

If You and I Believe in Christ 166

1 If you and I be-lieve in Christ and we to-geth-er pray,
2 If you and I re-main in Christ and we to-geth-er pray,
3 If you and I have faith in Christ and we to-geth-er pray,

the Ho - ly Spir - it will come down and set God's peo - ple free,
the Ho - ly Bi - ble teach - es us that God will hear our prayer,
the Ho - ly Spir - it shows us how to fol - low in God's way,

and set God's peo - ple free, and set God's peo - ple free;
that God will hear our prayer, that God will hear our prayer;
to fol - low in God's way, to fol - low in God's way,

the Ho - ly Spir - it will come down and set God's peo - ple free.
the Ho - ly Bi - ble teach - es us that God will hear our prayer.
the Ho - ly Spir - it shows us how to fol - low in God's way.

Words: st. 1 from Zimbabwe; st. 2-3, Bert Polman
Music: from Zimbabwe, as adapted from an English song
st. 2-3 © 2001, CRC Publications

167

Jesus, You Are Here with Me

Je - sus, you are here with me. Je - sus, you are

here with me. You hold me in your lov - ing arms. You

hold me in your lov - ing arms. You smile when I

call your name. You smile when I call your name. You

love to lis - ten when I pray. You love to lis - ten when I pray.

Lord, I Pray 168

Canon (st. 3)

1 Lord, I pray, if to-day some should wrong or
2 Should there be joy for me, help me thank you
3 If this day I should stray, show my heart the

trou-ble me, make me kind; bring to mind
as I should. Let me through all I do
road to take. Should I fear, please be near;

your for-give-ness makes me free.
praise you, Lord, for all things good.
hear my prayer for Je-sus' sake.

Canon accompaniment for keyboard, Orff, or other C instruments

Final ending

Words: Jean C. Keegstra-DeBoer, 1949, alt.
Music: Dutch melody; arr. Grace Schwanda, 1989
Arr. © 1994, CRC Publications

67 67
KLOKJE KLINKT

169

Let Us Pray

Let us pray, let us pray ev-ery-where and ev-

-ery way, ev-ery mo-ment of the day. It is the right

time. For the Fa-ther a-bove, he is

list-en-ing with love, and he wants to ans-wer us, so let us

pray.   Now let us pray.   Now let us pray.

Now let us pray.   Let us

Now   let us pray.

170 Lord, Listen to Your Children Praying

Lord, listen to your children praying,
Lord, send your Spirit in this place;
Lord, listen to your children praying,
send us love, send us power, send us grace!

Words and music: Ken Medema

PM
CHILDREN PRAYING

Morning Prayer

Lov - ing God, I of-fer you to - day
all that I think, I do, and I say. I
of - fer it all with all that was done by
Je - sus, my broth - er, Je - sus your Son.

172 What a Friend We Have in Jesus

Words: Joseph M. Scriven, 1855
Music: *The Sacred Harp*, Philadelphia, 1844; harm. A. Royce Eckhardt, 1972
Harm. © 1972, 1996, Covenant Publications

87 87D
BEACH SPRING

pain we bear, all be - cause we do not
sor - rows share? Je - sus knows our ev - ery
Lord in prayer! In his arms he'll take and

car - ry ev - ery - thing to God in prayer.
weak - ness; take it to the Lord in prayer.
shield you; you will find a so - lace there.

Siyabonga 173

Zulu Si - ya - bo - nga, Je - su. Si - ya - bo - nga, Je - su.
kiSwahili Asa - nte Ye - su, a - min. Asa - nte Ye - su, a - min.
siTswana Rea le - bo - ga, a - men. Rea le - bo - ga, a - men.
English Thank you, Je - sus, a - men. Thank you, Je - sus, a - men.

Si - ya - bo - nga, Je - su. Ha - le - lu - ya, a - men.
Asa - nte Ye - su, a - min. Ha - le - lu - ya, a - min.
Rea le - bo - ga, a - men. Ha - le - lu - ya, a - men.
Thank you, Je - sus, a - men. Al - le - lu - ia, a - men.

French

Merci, Jésus, amen. *(3x)*
Alléluia, amen.

German

Dank'sei dir, o Jesus. *(3x)*
Halleluya. Amen.

Spanish

Gracias, Jesús, amén. *(3x)*
Aleluya, amén.

Music: traditional Southern East African

174

The Lord's Prayer/Our Father

Capo 3

1 Our Father who art in hea - ven,
2 As in heav - en, so on the earth;
3 And for - give us, God, all our debts;
4 And lead us not in - to temp - ta - tion;

hal - low - ed be your name;

your king - dom come, your will be done.
give us this day our dai - ly bread.
as we for - give all our debt - ors.
but de - li - ver us from all e - vil.

Hal - low - ed be your name.

5 For yours is the kingdom, power, and glory;
  hallowed be your name;
  forever and forever and ever.
  Hallowed be your name.

6 Amen, amen, it shall be so;
  hallowed be your name;
  amen, amen, it shall be so.
  Hallowed be your name.

Music: traditional West Indian melody

Open Your Hearts

175

Words and music: Israeli folk song; tr. Carolyn Fritsch (20th c.); arr. Greg Scheer
Arr. © 2006, Faith Alive Christian Resources

9 8 9 5 refrain
YISRAEL V'ORAITA

176 Good News Medley

Good

news! Good news! Spread it all a-round.

Tell ev-ery-one of the treas-ure you have found. Good

news! Good news! Spread it near and far. More

3rd time to Coda

val-ua-ble than an-y-thing—the Bi-ble in your heart. Good

Words and music: Tony Salerno

177 Thy Word

Thy Word is a lamp un-to my feet and a light un-to my path.

1 When I feel a-fraid, think I've lost my way, still you're there right be-side me. And noth-ing will I fear as long as you are near.

2 I will not for-get your love for me, and yet my heart for-ev-er is wan-der-ing. Je-sus, be my guide and hold me to your side, and

Please be near me to the end.
I will love you to the end.

When We Wonder **178**

When we won-der, ask-ing ques-tions, teach us,

Lord, your learn-ing youth. Je - sus, help us

lis-ten close-ly to your wis-dom and your truth.

Words: Emily R. Brink, 1992
Music: Melody from *The Christian Lyre*, 1830; arr. Robert Roth, 1989
Words © 1994, CRC Publications. Arr. © 1989, Robert Roth. Used by permission.

87 87D
PLEADING SAVIOR

179 Open Our Eyes, Lord

How Great Is the Love of the Father

1 How great is the love of the Fa - ther, the
2 The world with-out God does not know us be -
3 What we are to be in the fu - ture as

love he has shown to us— so great that he
cause it did not know Christ. Lord, help us to
yet has not been made known, but when Christ re -

calls us his chil - dren, and chil - dren of God we
be pure and spot - less, for chil - dren of God we
turns, we shall see him, and then we shall be like

are, and chil - dren of God we are!
are, for chil - dren of God we are.
him, and then we shall be like him.

Words: 1 John 3:1-3; versified by Edna W. Sikkema, 1986
Music: James C. Ward, 1985; arr. Kathryn Tae Ritsema

97 97 with repeat
ANNO DOMINI

181 Baptized in Water

1 Bap - tized in wa - ter, sealed by the Spir - it,
2 Bap - tized in wa - ter, sealed by the Spir - it,
3 Bap - tized in wa - ter, sealed by the Spir - it,

cleansed by the blood of Christ, our King;
dead in the tomb with Christ, our King;
marked with the sign of Christ, our King;

heirs of sal - va - tion, trust - ing his prom - ise,
one with his ris - ing, freed and for - giv - en,
born of one Fa - ther, we are his chil - dren,

faith - ful - ly now God's praise we sing,
thank - ful - ly now God's praise we sing.
joy - ful - ly now God's praise we sing.

Words: Michael Saward
Music: Gaelic melody; arr. Norma de Waal Malefyt, 1992

558 D
BUNESSAN

Descant for "Baptized in Water"

I Am Crucified with Christ 182

183

You Are My All in All

Capo 3
Part 1

1 You are my strength when I am weak, you are the
2 Tak-ing my sin, my cross, my shame, ris-ing a-

trea-sure that I seek; you are my all in all.
gain— I bless your name; you are my all in all.

Seek-ing you as a pre-cious jewel, Lord, to give
When I fall down, you pick me up, when I am

up, I'd be a fool; you are my all in all.
dry, you fill my cup; you are my all in all.

Words and music: Dennis L. Jernigan

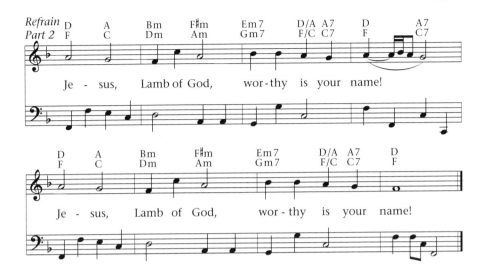

Refrain
Part 2

Je - sus,   Lamb of God,   wor-thy   is   your   name!

Je - sus,   Lamb of God,   wor-thy   is   your   name!

184 Lift Up Your Hearts/Sing Alleluia

Additional stanzas:

2 In Christ the world has been redeemed, . . .
3 His resurrection sets us free, . . .
4 Therefore we celebrate the feast, . . .
5 Sing alleluia to the Lord, . . .

Words: st. 1-4, early Christian liturgy; st. 5, Linda Stassen, 1974
Music: Linda Stassen, 1974; harm. Dale Grotenhuis, 1986
© 1974, Linda Stassen; © renewed 2002, Linda L. Benjamin, New Song Creations.
   All rights reserved. Used by permission.

Irregular
SING HALLELUJAH

When I Am Afraid 185

When I am a-fraid, I will trust in you, I will trust in you, I will trust in you. When I am a-fraid, I will trust in you, in God, whose word I praise.

God, whose word I praise.

186 Amazing Grace/Fill It Up

Capo 3

1 A - maz - ing grace— how sweet the sound— that
2 Twas grace that taught my heart to fear, and
3 The Lord has prom - ised good to me, his
4 Through man - y dan - gers, toils, and snares I
5 When we've been there ten thou - sand years, bright

saved a wretch like me! I once was lost but
grace my fears re - lieved; how pre - cious did that
word my hope se - cures; he will my shield and
have al - read - y come; 'tis grace hath brought me
shin - ing as the sun, we've no less days to

now am found, was blind but now I see.
grace ap - pear the hour I first be - lieved!
por - tion be as long as life en - dures.
safe thus far, and grace will lead me home.
sing God's praise than when we'd first be - gun.

Refrain

(So fill it up.) Fill it up and let it o - ver - flow. (So fill it

Words: John Newton, 1779
Music: traditional; arr. Joyce Borger
Arr. © 2006, Faith Alive Christian Resources

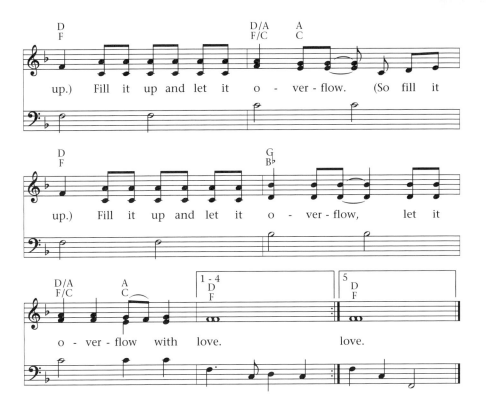

187 Be Still

Be still and know I am with you; still, for I will sus-

tain you; through-out your life I will al-ways be

near. Be still and know I am God.

To Coda on last refrain

1, 2, 3 Esus

To Stanzas Em

Stanzas Em

1 When life is scat-tered, I'm not far a-way.
2 When you are tempt-ed, es-cape you will see.
3 If you are thirst-y, come drink from the well.

Words and music: Richard K. Carson
© 1989, Hark! Productions, Inc.

Irregular
BE STILL

188 Don'na Tokidemo/ Anytime and Anywhere

Words: Junko Takahashi (1959-1966); tr. *Sing! A New Creation* (2001)
Music: Shin'ichi Takanami
© 2000, United Church of Christ in Japan; tr. © 2001, CRC Publications.
    Used by permission.

77 89 55 7
DON'NA TOKIDEMO

God's Path 189

Sometimes the path is hidden; we don't see where it goes. The future seems uncertain, but our God knows! We can't see where it is leading, but our God knows!

Words and music: Colleen Aalsburg Wiessner; harm. Joyce Borger
© 2006, Faith Alive Christian Resources

190

Give Me Oil in My Lamp

1 Give me oil in my lamp, keep me burn-ing.
2 Give me love in my heart, keep me shar-ing.
3 Give me joy in my heart, keep me sing-ing.
4 Give me faith in my heart, keep me pray-ing.

Give me oil in my lamp, I pray.
Give me love in my heart, I pray.
Give me joy in my heart, I pray.
Give me faith in my heart, I pray.

Give me oil in my lamp, keep me burn-ing.
Give me love in my heart, keep me shar-ing.
Give me joy in my heart, keep me sing-ing.
Give me faith in my heart, keep me pray-ing.

Keep me burn-ing till the break of day.
Keep me shar-ing till the break of day.
Keep me sing-ing till the break of day.
Keep me pray-ing till the break of day.

Words and music: traditional

Refrain

Sing ho-san-na, sing ho-san-na, sing ho-san-na to the King of kings! Sing ho-san-na, sing ho-san-na, sing ho-san-na to the King!

Jesus, I Love You 191

1 Je-sus, I *love you, love you, love you. Je-sus, I love you; Je-sus, my Lord. Lord.

*Additional stanzas:
2 serve, 3 praise, 4 pray to, 5 follow

Words and music: Otis Skillings; arr. Joseph Linn

192 The Lord Is My Shepherd

Alternative words: I'll follow him *or* I'll live for him

Second piano part, for playing as a duet:

Repeat through the entire song.
May also be played on Orff instruments.

Words: Psalm 23:1-2
Music: Folk melody; arr. Charlotte Larsen, 1992
Arr. © 1994, CRC Publications

Guide My Feet 193

Additional stanzas:

3 Stand by me while I run this race, . . .
4 I'm your child while I run this race, . . .
5 Search my heart while I run this race, . . .
6 Guide my feet while I run this race, . . .

Words and music: African-American spiritual; arr. Joyce Borger
Arr. © 2006, Faith Alive Christian Resources

8 8 8 10
GUIDE MY FEET

194 Great Is Thy Faithfulness

1 Great is thy faith - ful-ness, O God my Fa - ther;
2 Sum - mer and win - ter and spring-time and har - vest,
3 Par - don for sin and a peace that en - dur - eth,

there is no shad - ow of turn - ing with thee;
sun, moon, and stars in their cours - es a - bove
thy own dear pres - ence to cheer and to guide,

thou chang-est not, thy com - pas-sions, they fail not;
join with all na - ture in man - i - fold wit - ness
strength for to - day and bright hope for to - mor-row—

as thou hast been thou for - ev - er wilt be.
to thy great faith - ful-ness, mer - cy, and love.
bless - ings all mine, with ten thou-sand be - side!

Words: Thomas O. Chisholm
Music: William M. Runyan

11 10 11 10 with refrain
FAITHFULNESS

Refrain

Great is thy faith-ful-ness! Great is thy faith-ful-ness!

Morn - ing by morn - ing new mer - cies I see;

all I have need - ed thy hand hath pro - vid - ed.

Great is thy faith - ful-ness, Lord, un - to me!

195 God Is with Me

1 God is with me (a) ev - ery - where I go.
Ev - ery day and night I al - ways know
he (b) will nev - er leave; he prom - is - es to be
with me (a) ev - ery - where I go.

2 When (c) I am at church, at school, at home,
I know I (b) will nev - er be a - lone.
God (d) will al - ways be___ watch - ing o - ver me.
I (b) will nev - er be a - lone.

(a) With palm of hand facing up, spread arm around.
(b) Shake head no.
(c) Fingertips together to form point.
(d) Hands over eyebrows.

Words and music: Joy Sievers

God Is with Us

Words: Kathleen Hart Brumm, based on Matthew 1:23
© 1995, Kathleen Hart Brumm and Iteke Prins

197

God Knows Your Destination

1 At times it might seem real - ly hard
2 The Word of God heard yes - ter - day

fol - low - ing the Lord, but he'll be right there
is the same to - day. The Fa - ther has a

by your side, help - ing you to know that
plan for you; do not be a - fraid. For

God knows, God knows, God knows your

198 He Leadeth Me

1 He lead - eth me: O bless - ed thought! O
2 Lord, I would clasp thy hand in mine, nor
3 And when my task on earth is done, when,

words with heav - enly com - fort fraught! What -
ev - er mur - mur nor re - pine; con -
by thy grace, the vic - tory's won, e'en

e'er I do, wher - e'er I be, still
tent, what - ev - er lot I see, since
death's cold wave I will not flee, since

'tis God's hand that lead - eth me.
'tis my God that lead - eth me.
God through Jor - dan lead - eth me.

Refrain

He lead-eth me, he lead-eth me; by his own hand he

Words: Joseph H. Gilmore, 1862
Music: William B. Bradbury, 1864

LM with refrain
AUGHTON

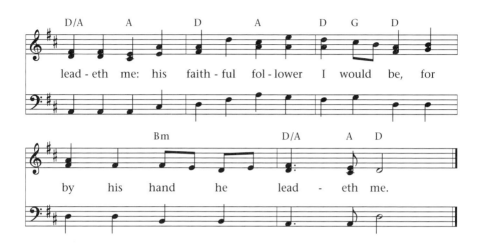

lead - eth me: his faith - ful fol - lower I would be, for
by his hand he lead - eth me.

God Is Watching over You 199

God is watch-ing o-ver you, watch-ing o - ver
you, watch-ing o - ver you. God is
watch-ing o-ver you, watch-ing o - ver you each day.

200 Hey-O

Capo 3

Refrain

Hey - o, hey - o, Je-sus is the way - o. Hey - o, hey - o,

Je-sus is the way. Hey - o, hey - o, Je-sus is the way - o.

Last time to Coda

Hey - o, hey - o, Je - sus is the way.

1 I'm hooked on Je - sus; he's my Lord, the
2 I'm hooked on Je - sus; he's the light, my
3 So ask the Lord in - to your heart; his

Words and music: Cheryl Thomas

ho - ly One that I a - dore. I'll fol - low him for
Lord, the way, the truth, the life. For - ev - er I will
love for you will nev - er part. Then heav - en - bound your

all my days. He's de - serv - ing of my praise.
lift his name. His righ - teous - ness I will pro - claim.
life will be. With him you'll live e - ter - nal - ly.

Je - sus is the way.

201 Humble Yourself in the Sight of the Lord

Words and music: Bob Hudson
© Maranatha! Music/CCCM Music (admin. Music Services).

If You're Happy 202

Substitute: stomp your feet
say "Amen"
do all three

203 I Am So Glad That Our Father in Heaven

Words and music: Philip P. Bliss, 1838-1876; arr. A. Royce Eckhardt
Arr. © 1996, A. Royce Eckhardt

10 10 10 10 with refrain
GLADNESS

The Counting Song 204

One, two, three, God takes care of me. Two, three, four, I love him more and more. Three, four, five, I'm glad he is a - live. Six, sev - en, eight, I think he's real - ly great. One, two, three, four, five, six, sev - en, eight. He's great!

205 I Walk by Faith

D.S. al Fine

me, tell me who can be a-gainst me? I

In Our Lives, Lord, Be Glorified 206

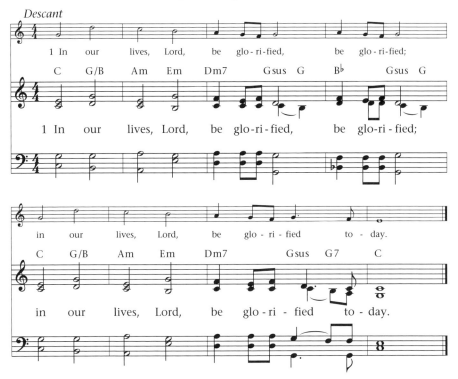

Descant

1 In our lives, Lord, be glo-ri-fied, be glo-ri-fied;

1 In our lives, Lord, be glo-ri-fied, be glo-ri-fied;

in our lives, Lord, be glo-ri-fied to-day.

in our lives, Lord, be glo-ri-fied to-day.

Additional stanzas:

2 In our homes, Lord, . . .
3 In your church, Lord, . . .
4 In your world, Lord, . . .

207 I Want to Walk as a Child of the Light

1 I want to walk as a child of the light;
2 I want to see the bright-ness of God;
3 I'm look-ing for the com-ing of Christ;

I want to fol - low Je - sus.
I want to look at Je - sus.
I want to be with Je - sus.

God set the stars to give light to the world; the
Clear Sun of righ-teous-ness, shine on my path, and
When we have run with pa - tience the race, we

star of my life is Je - sus.
show me the way to the Fa - ther.
shall know the joy of Je - sus.

Words and music: Kathleen Thomerson
© 1970, 1975, Celebration

10 7 10 8 with refrain
HOUSTON

208 In Christ Alone

1 In Christ a-lone my hope is found; he is my light, my strength, my song— this cor-ner-stone, this sol-id ground, firm through the fierc-est drought and storm. What heights of

2 In Christ a-lone, who took on flesh— full-ness of God in help-less babe!— this gift of love and right-eous-ness, scorned by the ones he came to save. 'Til on the

3 There in the ground his bod-y lay, light of the world by dark-ness slain; then, burst-ing forth in glo-ri-ous day, up from the grave he rose a-gain! And as he

4 No guilt in life, no fear in death, this is the pow'r of Christ in me; from life's first cry to fi-nal breath, Je-sus com-mands my des-ti-ny. No pow'r of

209 Jesus Loves Me

1 Je - sus loves me, this I know, for the Bi - ble tells me so.
2 Je - sus loves me— he who died, heav-en's gate to o - pen wide.
3 Je - sus loves me, this I know, as he loved so long a - go,

Lit - tle ones to him be-long; they are weak, but he is strong.
He will wash a - way my sin, let his lit - tle child come in.
tak - ing chil-dren on his knee, say - ing, "Let them come to me."

Refrain

Yes, Je - sus loves me! Yes, Je - sus loves me!

Yes, Je - sus loves me! The Bi - ble tells me so.

Japanese:
1 Saq ware wo aisu,
   saq wa tsuyo kere ba,
   ware yowaku-pomo,
   osore wa araji.
   Waga shu Iesu, *(3x)*
   Ware wo aisu.

Spanish:
1 Cristo me␣ama, bien lo sé
   Su palabra me hace ver
   Que los niños son de␣Aquel
   Quien es nuestro␣Amigo fiel
   Si, Cristo me␣ama, *(3x)*
   La Biblia dice así.

Words: st. 1-2, Anna B. Warner, 1859; st. 3, David R. McGuire, 1971;
   Japanese tr. Mas Kawashima; Spanish tr. *Himnarió Metodísta*
Music: William B. Bradbury, 1861; arr. Horace Boyer
Japanese tr. © 1989, United Methodist Publishing House (admin. The Copyright Co.).
   All rights reserved. International copyright secured. Used by permission.

77 77 with refrain
JESUS LOVES ME

One, Two, Three, Jesus Loves Me 210

One, two, three, Je-sus loves me. One, two, Je-sus loves you. Three, four, he loves you more than you've ev-er been loved be-fore. Five, six, seven, we're go-ing to heaven. Eight, nine, it's tru-ly di-vine. Nine, ten, it's time to end; but in-stead we'll sing it a-gain. there's no time to sing it a-gain.

Words and music: Lisa Mazak
© 1974, 1975, Celebration. All rights reserved. Used by permission.

211

May the Mind of Christ, My Savior

Words: 1-4 Kate B. Wilkinson, 1925; alt. refrain Greg Scheer (based on Wilkinson, st. 5)
Music: Greg Scheer
Music © 2000, Greg Scheer.

87 85

weighs our souls, look - ing on - ly un - to Je - sus

as our source and goal. May the goal. *rit.*

212 Sandy Land

Don't build your house on the sand - y land; don't build it too near the shore. Well, it might look kind of nice, but you'll have to build it twice; oh, you'll have to build your house once more. You'd bet - ter build your house up - on a rock. Make a

good foun - da - tion on a sol - id spot. Oh, the

storms may come and go, but the

peace of God you will know.

Rock of ag - es, cleft for me,

let me hide my - self in thee.

213 Stand on the Rock

214 **We Believe**

1 We be-lieve in God the Fath-er, ma-ker of the
2 We be-lieve he sends his Spir-it on his church with

un - i - verse. And in Christ, the Son, our Sav - ior,
gifts of power. God, his word of truth af - firm-ing,

come to us by vir - gin birth. We be - lieve he
sends us to the na - tions now. He will come a -

died to save us, bore our sins, was cru - ci - fied;
gain in glor - y— judge the liv - ing and the dead;

then from death, he rose vic - tor - ious as-cend - ed to the
ev - 'ry knee shall bow be - fore him; then must ev - 'ry

Words and music: Graham Kendrick

Je - sus, Lord of all, Lord of all.

Lord of all. Lord of all.

We Love **215**

We love (clap, clap) be-cause God first loved us. We
love (clap, clap) be-cause God first loved us. We
love, (clap, clap) we love, (clap, clap) we love (clap,
clap) be-cause God first (clap) loved (clap) us. (clap, clap)

Words: 1 John 4:19
Music: Ann F. Price

216

Trust in the Lord with All Your Heart

Nah nah nah nah nah nah—

Trust in the Lord with all your heart.

Lean not on your own un - der - stand - ing.

In all your ways ac-know - ledge him, and he will make your

paths straight.

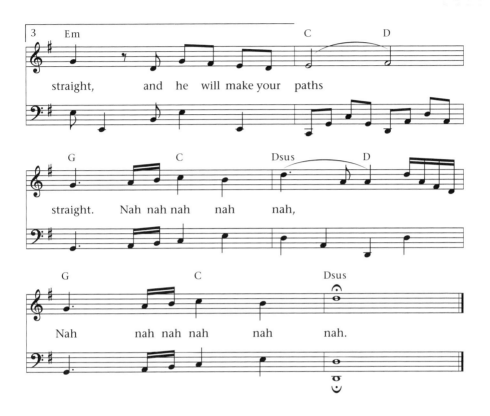

217 **Walk Like Jesus**

218 Trust and Obey

Capo 3

When we walk with the Lord in the light of his
While we do his good will he a - bides with us

Word, what a glo - ry he sheds on our way!
still, and with all who will

trust and o - bey. Trust and o - bey, for there's no oth - er

way to be hap - py in Je - sus but to trust and o - bey.

Words: John H. Sammis, 1887
Music: Daniel B. Towner, 1887

669 D with refrain
TRUST AND OBEY

Through It All 219

Capo 1

Through it all, through it all, I've learned to trust in Je - sus; I've learned to trust in God. Through it all, through it all, I've learned to de-pend up - on God's Word.

Words and music: Andraé Crouch

220 You Shall Love the Lord

221 Yes, Lord, Yes

Words and music: Lynn Keesecker

Jesus' Hands Were Kind Hands 222

1 Je - sus' hands were kind hands, do - ing good to all,
2 Take my hands, Lord Je - sus, let them work for you;

heal - ing pain and sick - ness, bless - ing chil - dren small,
make them strong and gen - tle, kind in all I do.

wash - ing ti - red feet and sav - ing those who fall;
Let me watch you, Je - sus, till I'm gen - tle too,

Je - sus' hands were kind hands, do - ing good to all.
till my hands are kind hands, quick to work for you.

Words: Margaret Cropper, c. 1926
Music: traditional French melody
Words © 1979, Stainer & Bell, Ltd. (admin. Hope Publishing Company).
    All rights reserved. Used by permission.

11 11 11 11
AU CLAIR DE LA LUNE

223 Lord, Make Me an Alleluia

May be sung in canon

1 Lord, make me an al - le - lu - ia; Lord, make me an al - le - lu - ia; Lord, make me an al - le - lu - ia, from head to toe!

2 Lord, make me a faith - ful ser - vant; Lord, make me a faith - ful ser - vant; Lord, make me a faith - ful ser - vant, from head to toe!

3 Lord, make me a friend to oth - ers; Lord, make me a friend to oth - ers; Lord, make me a friend to oth - ers, from head to toe!

Handbell or Orff instrument ostinati

Words: Rae E. Whitney (based on words of Augustine of Hippo), 1987
Music: Ray W. Urwin, 1994

85 85
ALLELUIA ME FACE

Make Me a Servant 224

Make me a ser - vant, hum - ble and meek.

Lord, let me lift up those who are weak.

And may the prayer of my heart al - ways be:

Make me a ser - vant, make me a ser - vant,

make me a ser - vant to - day.

225 Enviado soy de Dios/ Sent Out in Jesus' Name

Capo 1

Spanish En - via - do soy de Dios, mi ma - no lis - ta es - tá
English Sent out in Je - sus' name, our hands are rea - dy now

pa - ra cons - tru - ir con El un mun - do fra - ter - nal.
to make the earth the place in which the king-dom comes.

Los án - ge - les no son en - via - dos a cam - biar un
The an - gels can - not change a world of hurt and pain in -

mun - do de do - lor por un mun - do de paz. Me
to a world of love, of jus - tice and of peace. The

Words: anonymous, from Cuba; English tr. Jorge E. Maldonado; arr. Carmen Pena

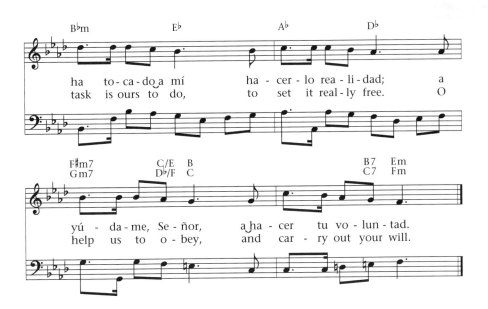

226 Take My Life

1 Take my life that it may be all you
2 Take my hands and let them move at the
3 Take my voice and let me sing al - ways,
4 Take my love; my Lord, I pour at your

pur - pose, Lord, for me. Take my mo - ments
im - pulse of your love. Take my feet and
on - ly, for my King. Take my lips and
feet its trea - sure store. Take my - self, and

and my days; let them sing your end - less praise.
lead their way; nev - er let them go a - stray.
keep them true, filled with mes - sag - es from you.
I will be yours for all e - ter - ni - ty.

Words: Frances R. Havergal, 1874; revised for *Psalter Hymnal*, 1987
Music: Timothy Hoekman, 1979
Music © 1985, CRC Publications

77 77
TEBBEN

Take, Oh, Take Me as I Am 227

Take, O take me as I am; sum-mon out what I shall be;

set your seal up-on my heart and live in me.

Words and music: John Bell
© 1995, Wild Goose Resource Group, Iona Community, Scotland. GIA Publications, Inc., exclusive North American agent. All rights reserved. Used by permission.

Thuma Mina/ Send Me, Lord 228

Zulu Thu - ma mi - na, thu - ma mi - na,
English Send me, Lord, send me, Lord,

Leader Thu - ma mi - na

thu - ma mi - na Nko - si yam.
send me, Lord, in - to the world.

Additional stanzas:

Lead me, Lord . . . into the world.
Teach me, Lord . . . your holy Word.

Words and music: traditional, South Africa; tr. David Dargie
Music transcription © 1983, David Dargie; admin. Choristers Guild

229 You Are My Shepherd

230 Now Thank We All Our God

Words: Martin Rinkart, 1636; tr. Catherine Winkworth, 1863
Music: Johann Cruger, 1647

67 67 66 66
NUN DANKET

Go Now in Peace

231

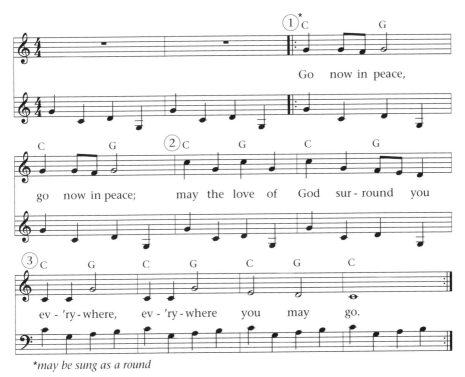

Go now in peace,
go now in peace; may the love of God sur-round you
ev-'ry-where, ev-'ry-where you may go.

*may be sung as a round

Alto glockenspiel   Alto xylophone

Metallophone   Bass xylophone

232 As You Go on Your Way

Go Ye, Go Ye into the World

233

1 Go ye, go ye in-to the world, and
2 Go ye, go ye in-to the world, and
3 Go ye, go ye in-to the world, and

make dis-ci-ples of all the na-tions.
take the gos-pel to all the peo-ple.
tell the sto-ry to all be-liev-ers.

Refrain

Go ye, go ye in-to the world, and

I will be with you there!

Words and music: Natalie Sleeth, based on Matthew 28:19-20; adapted from the anthem
   "Go into the World."
© 1979, Choristers Guild

234 My Friends, May You Grow in Grace

My friends, may you grow in grace and in the knowl-edge of our Lord and Sav - ior. My friends, may you grow in grace and in the knowl-edge of Je - sus Christ. To God be the glo-ry, now and for-ev - er,

Words and music: Timothy James Meaney and Sean Diamond; revised by Gregg De Mey and Gregory Kett
© 1991, 2001, Wiseman Music. Used by permission.

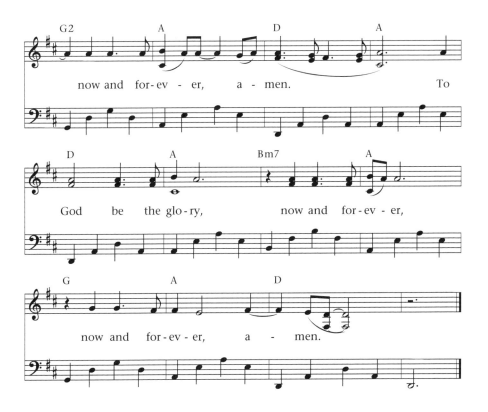

235 Somos uno en Cristo/
We Are One in Christ Jesus

Spanish So - mos u - no en Cris - to, so - mos u - no, so - mos
English We are one in Christ Je - sus, all one bod - y, all one

u - no, u - no só - lo. só - lo. Un so - lo
spir - it, all to - geth - er. geth - er. We share one

Dios, un so - lo Se - ñor, u - na so - la fe,
God, one might - y Lord, one a - bid - ing faith,

un so - lo a - mor, un so - lo bau - tis - mo, un so - lo Es -
one bind - ing love, one sin - gle bap - ti - sm, one Ho - ly

pí - ri - tu y é - se es el Con - so - la - dor.
Com - fort - er, the Ho - ly Spir - it, u - nit - ing all.

Words and music: anonymous; tr. Alice Parket; arr. Philip W. Blycker   SOMOS UNO
© 1996, Abingdon Press (admin. The Copyright Co.); arr. © 1992, Celebremos/Libros Alianza.
    All rights reserved. International copyright secured. Used by permission.

Bring Forth the Kingdom 236

237 Behold, What Manner of Love

Words and music: Patricia Van Tine, based on 1 John 3:1

I'm Gonna Live So God Can Use Me 238

Capo 3

1 I'm gon-na *live so (*live so) God can use me an-y-where, Lord, an-y-time! (an-y-time)

I'm gon-na *live so (*live so) God can use me an-y-where, Lord, an-y-time! (an-y-time)

Additional stanzas: work, play, sing, *etc.*

Words and music: African-American spiritual; arr. Joyce Borger, 2005
Arr. © 2006, Faith Alive Christian Resources

239 Bind Us Together

Bind us to-geth-er, Lord, bind us to-geth-er with cords that can-not be bro - ken.

Bind us to-geth-er, Lord, bind us to-geth-er, bind us to-geth-er in love.

There is on - ly one God.

240 I Love to Tell the Story

1 I love to tell the sto - ry of un - seen things a - bove, of
2 I love to tell the sto - ry; 'tis pleas - ant to re - peat what
3 I love to tell the sto - ry, for those who know it best seem

Je - sus and his glo - ry, of Je - sus and his love. I
seems, each time I tell it, more won - der - ful - ly sweet. I
hun - ger-ing and thirst -ing to hear it, like the rest, and

love to tell the sto - ry be - cause I know 'tis true; it
love to tell the sto - ry, for some have nev - er heard the
when, in scenes of glo - ry, I sing the new, new song, 'twill

sat - is - fies my long-ings as noth - ing else can do.
mes - sage of sal - va - tion from God's own ho - ly Word.
be the old, old, sto - ry that I have loved so long.

Words and music: William G. Fischer, 1869; arr. Kathryn Tae Ritsema
Arr. © 2006, Faith Alive Christian Resources

76 76 D with refrain
HANKEY

I love to tell the sto-ry; 'twill be my theme in glo-ry to

tell the old, old sto-ry of Je-sus and his love.

Friends Love One Another 241

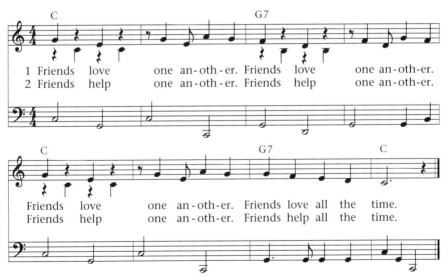

1 Friends love one an-oth-er. Friends love one an-oth-er.
2 Friends help one an-oth-er. Friends help one an-oth-er.

Friends love one an-oth-er. Friends love all the time.
Friends help one an-oth-er. Friends help all the time.

242 Stop! And Let Me Tell You

1 Stop! and let me tell you what the Lord has done for
2 Go! and tell the sto - ry of the Christ of Cal - va -
3 Watch! and be read - y, for the Lord may come to -

me. Stop! and let me tell you what the
ry. Go! and tell the sto - ry of the
day. Watch! and be read - y, for the

Lord has done for me. He for - gave my sin and he
Christ of Cal - va - ry. He'll for - give their sins; he will
Lord may come to - day. He will come a - gain in the

saved my soul; he cleansed my heart and he made me whole.
save their souls; he'll cleanse their hearts; he will make them whole.
clouds for me and take me home for e - ter - ni - ty.

Stop! and let me tell you what the Lord has done for me.
Go! and tell the sto - ry of the Christ of Cal - va - ry.
Watch! and be read - y, for the Lord may come to - day.

Words: st. 1, unknown; st. 2, Reider Kalland; st. 3, Wallace Grant
Music: unknown; arr. Larry Haron

Lift High the Cross 243

1 Come, Chris-tians, fol-low where our Sav-ior led, our
2 All new-born ser-vants of the Cru-ci-fied bear
3 O Lord, once lift-ed on the tree of pain, draw
4 Let ev-ery race and ev-ery lan-guage tell of

King vic-to-rious, Je-sus Christ, our Head.
on their brows the seal of him who died.
all the world to seek you once a-gain.
him who saves our lives from death and hell.

Words: George W. Kitchin; revised by Michael R. Newbolt
Music: Sydney H. Nicholson; arr. Robert Roth

10 10 with refrain
CRUCIFER

244 There's No God as Great/ No hay Dios tan grande

English There's no god as great as you, O Lord, O Lord, my God.
Spanish No hay dios tan gran-de co-mo tú, no lo hay, no lo hay.

There's no god who works the might-y won-ders, all the
No hay dios que pue-da ha-cer las o-bras co-mo

won - ders that you do. do. Not by our
las que ha-ces tú. tú. No es con es -

weap-ons, nor by our pow - er, but by your Spir - it we are
pa - da, ni con e - jér - ci-to, mas con tu San-to Es-pí - ri-

Words and music: Spanish; tr. for *Psalter Hymnal,* 1987

NO HAY DIOS

245 This Little Light of Mine

1 This lit-tle light of mine, I'm gon-na let it
shine; this lit-tle light of mine,
I'm gon-na let it shine, let it shine, let it
shine, let it shine.

2 Hide it un-der a
3 Don't let an-y-one
4 Share my light with

bas - ket? No! I'm gon-na let it shine.
(blow) it out. I'm gon-na let it shine.
oth - ers! Yes! I'm gon-na let it shine.

F

Hide it un-der a bas-ket? No! I'm gon-na let it
Don't let an-y-one *(blow)* it out. I'm gon-na let it
Share my light with oth-ers! Yes! I'm gon-na let it

C   G   C

shine, let it shine, let it shine, let it shine.
shine, let it shine, let it shine, let it shine.
shine, let it shine, let it shine, let it shine.

246 We Are the Church

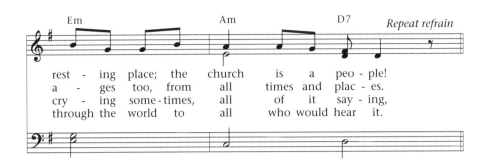

rest - ing place; the church is a peo - ple!
a - ges too, from all times and plac - es.
cry - ing some - times, all of it say - ing,
through the world to all who would hear it.

Hine Ma Tov 247

May be sung as a round

Hi - ne ma to - vu ma na - im she-vet a - him gam ya - chad.

Hi - ne ma - to she-vet a - him gam ya - chad.

*How very good and pleasant it is
when kindred live together in unity!
Psalm 133:1, NRSV*

Words: Psalm 133:1
Music: traditional Israeli; arr. Greg Scheer
Arr. © 2006, Faith Alive Christian Resources

248 You and I

Capo 1

1 Who's goin' to tell the sto - ry? You and I!
2 Who's goin' to bring the king-dom? You and I!
4 Who's goin' to feed the hun - gry? You and I!

Tell of the Lord's great glo - ry? You and I!
Who's goin' to spread the gos-pel? You and I!
Care for the sick and lone-ly? You and I!

Who's goin' to let the whole world know?
Who's goin' to do the kind - ly deed?
Who's goin' to let the whole world see

Help his dis - ci - ples grow and mul - ti - ply?
Com-fort the one in need and help sup - ply?
peo - ple can live in har - mo - ny? Let's try!

249 Jesu, Jesu, Fill Us with Your Love

Copyright Holders

Each song under copyright, whether text, tune, or arrangement, is indicated as such at the bottom of the first page of each song. If you wish to reproduce (or reprint) any copyrighted words or music contained in this book, please contact the copyright holder for permission.

A. Royce Eckhardt
242 Essex Place
Wilmette IL 60091
Phone: 847-446-7777

Abingdon Press
1025 16th Ave South - Suite 204
Nashville TN 37212
Phone: 615-321-1096
Fax: 615-321-1099

Augsburg Fortress Publishers
PO Box 1209
Minneapolis MN 55440-1209
Phone: 800-421-0239
Fax: 612-330-3252

BMG Music, Inc.
8750 Wilshire Blvd
Beverly Hills CA 90211
Phone: 310-358-4767
Fax: 310-358-4765

Brentwood Benson
8750 Wilshire Blvd
Beverly Hills CA 90211
Phone: 310-358-4767
Fax: 310-358-4765

Bridge Building Music/
    Nilsson Media Ministry
8750 Wilshire Blvd
Beverly Hills CA 90211
Phone: 310-358-4767
Fax: 310-358-4765

Broadman & Holman Publishers
127 9th Ave North
Nashville TN 37234
Phone: 615-251-2000
Fax: 615-251-2701

Brummhart Publishing
708 Blooming Grove Dr
Renssalaer NY 12144
Phone: 518-286-2910
Fax: 518-286-1837

Celebration
PO Box 309
Aliquippa PA 37212
Phone: 615-321-1096
Fax: 615-321-1099

Celebremos/Libros Alianza
A. A. 100
Cucuta
Columbia
Phone: 577-574-2959
Fax: 577-574-4328

Charlie Monk Music
c/o Alfred Publishing Co.
15800 Northwest 48th Ave
Miami FL 33014
Phone: 305-521-1681
Fax: 305-625-3480

Chorister's Guild
2834 W Kingsley Rd
Garland TX 75041
Phone: 972-271-1521
Fax: 972-840-3113

Christian Conference of Asia
Pak Tin Village, Mei Tin Road
Shatin N.T.
Hong Kong
Phone: 852-26911068
Fax: 852-26924378
email cca@cca.org.hk

Concordia Publishing House
3558 South Jefferson Ave
St Louis MO 63118
Phone: 800-325-0191
Fax: 314-268-1329

CRC Publications
See Faith Alive Christian Resources

Daybreak Music
1000 Cody Rd
Mobile AL 36695
Phone: 251-633-9000
Fax: 251-776-5036

Dayspring Music
20 Music Square East
Nashville TN 37203
Phone: 615-733-1880
Fax: 615-733-1885

Designer Music
See Brentwood Benson

Dosia Carlson
555 W- Glendale Ave.
Phoenix AZ 85021
Phone: 602-995-4134

E. C. Schirmer
138 Ipswich St
Boston MA 2215
Phone: 617-236-1935

Editora Sinodal
Caixa Postal 11
93001 Sao Leopoldo, R.S.
Brazil
Phone: 011-55-51-590-2366
Fax: 011-55-51-590-2366

EMI Christian Music Publishing
PO Box 5085
101 Winners Circle
Brentwood TN 37029
Phone: 615-371-4400
Fax: 615-371-6897

Ever Devoted Music,
    c/o Willow Creek Association
PO Box 3188
Barrington IL 60011-3188
Phone: 847-765-0070
Fax: 847-765-5046

Faith Alive Christian Resources
2850 Kalamazoo Ave SE
Grand Rapids MI 49560
Phone: 616-224-0784
Fax: 616-224-0834
permissions@FaithAliveResources.org

Gaither Copyright Management
PO Box 737
Alexandria IN 46001
Fax: 765-724-8290

Gerhard M. Cartford
2279 Commonwealth Ave
St. Paul MN 55108

GIA Publications
7404 South Mason Ave
Chicago IL 60638
Phone: 800-442-1358
Fax: 708-496-3828
www.giamusic.com

Gospel Light
1957 Eastman Ave
Ventura CA 93003
Phone: 805-644-9721
Fax: 805-644-9728

Greg Leavers
1 Haws Hill
Carnforth Lancs. LA5 9DD
United Kingdom

Greg Scheer
3650 Ridgeway Rd SE
Grand Rapids MI 49546
Phone: 616-464-1505
www.gregscheer.com

Group Publishing, Inc
Dept BK. Box 481
Loveland CO 80539
Phone: 970-292-4278
Fax: 970-292-4360

Hal Leonard Corporation
7777 West Bluemound Road
PO Box 13819
Milwaukee WI 53213
Phone: 414-774-3630
Fax: 414-774-3259

Hark! Productions
2200 Tart Lake Rd
Lino Lakes MN 55038
Phone: 651-653-5211

Hinshaw Music
PO Box 470
Chapel Hill NC 27514
Phone: 919-933-1691
Fax: 919-967-3399

Hope Publishing
380 South Main Place
Carol Stream IL 60188
Phone: 800-323-1049
Fax: 630-665-2552
www.hopepublishing.com

Integrated Copyright Group
PO Box 24149
Nashville TN 37202
Phone: 615-329-3999
Fax: 615-329-4070

Integrity Music
1000 Cody Rd
Mobile AL 36695
Phone: 251-633-9000
Fax: 251-776-5036

Jimmy and Gail Getzen
181 Jones Lane
Hendersonville TN 37075
Phone: 615-822-0633

Jonathan Malicsi
Faculty Center
UP Diliman
1101 Quezon City
Philippines
Phone: 926-9887 or
    920-5301 loc 7419
Fax: 927-1928
mlcsjon@philonline.com

Kathleen and Scott Tunseth
797 Sextant Ave W
Roseville MN 55113
Phone: 651-481-7903

Lawrence M Probes
PO Box 788
Traverse City MI 49685-0788

Lifeway Christian Resources
One Lifeway Plaza
Nashville TN 37234
Phone: 615-251-2000
Fax: 615-251-3727

Lorenz Publishing
501 East Third Street
PO Box 802
Dayton OH 45401
Phone: 800-444-1144
Fax: 937-223-2042

Manna Music, Inc.
35255 Brooten Road
Pacific City OR 97135
Phone: 503-965-6112
Fax: 503-965-6880

Maranatha! Music
1526 Otter Creek Rd
Nashville TN 37215
Phone: 615-371-1320
Fax: 615-371-1351

Marie Jo Thum
8549 Eagle Run Drive
Boca Raton FL 33434
Phone: 561-482-2067

Marilyn Houser Hamm
600 Shaftesbury
Winnepeg MB R3P 0M4
Canada

MaryLu Walker
16 Brown Road
Corning NY 14830
marluwalk@stny.rr.com

Matterhorn Music
8611 Poinsettia Dr
Temple Terrace FL 33637
Phone: 813-980-0200
Fax: 813-988-3134

Meadowgreen Group
1526 Otter Creek Rd
Nashville TN 37215
Phone: 615-371-1320
Fax: 615-371-1351

Mercy/Vineyard Publishing
1526 Otter Creek Rd
Nashville TN 37215
Phone: 615-371-1320
Fax: 615-371-1351

Mission Hills Music
PO Box 470787
Charlotte NC 28247
Phone: 800-992-7711
Alternate Number 704-362-1007

Momcat Productions
1124 Aberdeen Road
Inverness IL 60067
Phone: 847-705-8110

Music Anno Domini
James Ward
4106 St Elmo Ave
Chattanooga TN 37409
Phone: 423-821-1315

Music Services
1526 Otter Creek Rd
Nashville TN 37215
Phone: 615-371-1320
Fax: 615-371-1351

New Song Creations
PO Box 308
Erin TN 37061
Phone: 931-289-3853

New Spring Publishing
8750 Wilshire Blvd
Beverly Hills CA 90211
Phone: 310-358-4701
Fax: 310-358-4765

Nobuaki Hanaoka
6929 Franklin Blvd
Sacramento CA 95823

OCP Publications
5536 NE Hassalo
Portland OR 97213
Phone: 503-281-1191
Fax: 503-282-3486

Paideia Press
PO Box 1000
Jordan Station ON L0R 1S0
Canada
Phone: 905-562-5719
Fax: 905-562-7828
christianrenewal@hotmail.com

Price Stern Sloan Publishers
375 Hudson St
New York NY 10014
Phone: 212-414-3553
Fax: 212-366-2680

Richard Smallwood
107 Hemlock Court
Hendersonville TN 37075
Phone: 615-822-5308

Robert Roth
330 Morgan St
Oberlin OH 44074

ROM Administration
PO 1252
Fairhope AL 36533
Phone: 251-929-2411
Fax: 251-929-2404

Scarlet Moon Music
PO Box 320
Pegram TN 37143
Phone: 615-952-3999
Fax: 615-952-3151

Selah Publishing
PO Box 98066
Pittsburgh PA 15227
Phone: 412-886-1020
Fax: 412-886-1022
licensing@selahpub.com

Silliman University Music
Ulahingan Research Project
Dumaguete City 6200
Philippines
Phone: 035-422-8880
Fax: 011-063-422-8880
www.su.edu.ph

Sparrow
1526 Otter Creek Rd
Nashville TN 37215
Phone: 615-371-1321

St. Christophers College
815 Second Ave
New York NY 10017

Stephan Hopkinson
2 S. Swithen St
Winchester S023 9JP
England

Susan Mulder Langeland
2530 Argus Ave SE
Grand Rapids MI 49546
Phone: 616-975-9810

The Copyright Company
1025 16th Ave South - Suite 204
Nashville TN 37212
Phone: 615-321-1096
Fax: 615-321-1099

The Covenant Press
5101 N. Francisco Ave
Chicago IL 60625
Phone: 773-784-3000
Fax: 773-784-4366

The Hymn Society
380 South Main Place
Carol Stream IL 60188
Phone: 800-323-1049
Fax: 630-665-2552

United Church of Christ - Japan
2-3-18 Nishiwaseda
Shinjuku-ku Toyko 169-0051
Japan
Phone: 81-03-3203-0372
Fax: 81-03-3204-9495

United Methodist Publishing
1025 16th Ave South - Suite 204
Nashville TN 37212
Phone: 615-321-1096
Fax: 615-321-1099

Universal Music Corp., Sound III, Inc.
7777 West Bluemound Road
PO Box 13819
Milwaukee WI 53213
Phone: 414-774-3630
Fax: 414-774-3259

Wiseman Music
PO Box 7494
Bellevue WA 98008
Phone: 425-401-8844
Fax: 425-644-8160

Word Music Group, Inc.
20 Music Square East
Nashville TN 37215
Phone: 615-733-1880
Fax: 615-733-1885

World Council of Churches
PO Box 2100
150 route de Ferney
CH-1211 Geneva 2
Switzerland
Phone: 41-22-791-6111
Fax: 011-41-22-791-0361

Worshiptogether.com
1526 Otter Creek Rd
Nashville TN 37215
Phone: 615-371-1320
Fax: 615-371-1351

Ylvisaker, Inc.
Box 321
Waverly IA 50677
Phone: 319-352-4396
Fax: 319-352-0765

Capo Chart

Pianists may find "flat" keys easier to play than "sharp" keys. But the opposite is true for guitarists. Using a capo to clamp the strings allows a guitarist to transpose to a more convenient key. Shortening the strings by one fret (Capo 1) will raise the pitch a half step; clamping on the third fret (Capo 3) will raise the pitch three half steps.

The chart below shows how a capo can be used to play in more convenient keys. For example, by using Capo 3, a song in the key of F (with one flat) can be played as if in the key of D. The resulting sound from the shortened strings will actually be in F. All major and minor chords are listed.

Capo suggestions are made at the beginnings of many songs. For those songs, find the key signature and key below, add the capo, and play the chords in parentheses. The resulting sound will be in the original key.

| Number of flats | Scale degree | | | | | | |
	1	2	3	4	5	6	7
Key of F capo 3	F (D)	Gm (Em)	Am (F#m)	B♭ (G)	C (A)	Dm (Bm)	
Key of F capo 5	F (C)	Gm (Dm)	Am (Em)	B♭ (F)	C (G)	Dm (Am)	
Key of Dm capo 5	Dm (Am)		F (C)	Gm (Dm)	A (E)	B♭ (F)	C (G)
Key of B♭ capo 1	B♭ (A)	Cm (Bm)	Dm (C#m)	E♭ (D)	F (E)	Gm (F#m)	
Key of E♭ capo 1	E♭ (D)	Fm (Em)	Gm (F#m)	A♭ (G)	B♭ (A)	Cm (Bm)	
Key of E♭ capo 3	E♭ (C)	Fm (Dm)	Gm (Em)	A♭ (F)	B♭ (G)	Cm (Am)	
Key of Cm capo 5	Cm (Gm)		E♭ (B♭)	Fm (Cm)	G (D)	A♭ (E♭)	B♭ (F)
Key of A♭ capo 1	A♭ (G)	Bbm (Am)	Cm (Bm)	D♭ (C)	E♭ (D)	Fm (Em)	
Key of Fm capo 1	Fm (Em)		A♭ (G)	B♭m (Am)	C (B)	D♭ (C)	E♭ (D)

Key to Music Terms, Symbols, and Abbreviations

alt.   altered

arr.   arrangement, arranged by

c.   for Latin word (*circa* = "around") meaning "around a certain date"

Capo   for guitarists, to indicate an alternative key; see chart on page 361

CM   common meter (poetry in four-line stanzas, each with the following number of syllables: 8, 6, 8, 6)

CMD   common meter double (eight lines: 8, 6, 8, 6, 8, 6, 8, 6 or 86868686)

Coda   Italian word meaning "the closing section of a song"

Da Capo   Italian words for "the head," meaning "go back to the beginning"

D.C.   short form for *Da Capo*

D.S.   short form for Italian words *Dal Segno,* meaning "return to %"

Fine   Italian word meaning "the end" (pronounced "FEE-nay"); this is where the song ends.

harm.   harmonization, harmonized by

LM   long meter (poetry in four-line stanzas, each with eight syllables)

LMD   long meter double (eight lines)

N.C.   no chord (guitar)

SM   short meter (poetry in four-line stanzas, each with the following number of syllables: 6,6,8,6)

SMD   short meter double (eight lines: 6, 6, 8, 6, 6, 6, 8, 6 or 66866686)

st.   stanza(s)

tr.   translation, translated by

%   symbol for *segno* ("sign"); this is where you need to return to when you reach the instructions *D.C. al* % or *D.S.*

Index of First Lines and Titles